About

Shiv Sengupta experienced a powerful awakening in his twenties after suffering from years of debilitating depression. What followed was an unexpected four-month period of inner silence and psychological freedom which, to his disappointment, eventually ebbed. After spending several frustrating years attempting to recreate his experience, he realized that awakening wasn't a solution in itself, but a glimpse into an effective way of approaching the problem of our existence. A problem that he spent the next decade investigating without resorting to metaphysical rationalizations, spiritual belief systems or cut-and-dried scientific explanations.

He came to realize that his 'own mind' wasn't the problem, as he had once been led to believe. The problem was that his mind wasn't his own to begin with. It belonged to others—to society, to peer groups and to political, social and spiritual authority figures. And in order to reclaim his mind, he embarked on a process of painstakingly questioning his beliefs—from the personal to the social, from the metaphysical to the mundane.

In 2018, Shiv began sharing his reflections on a Facebook page called *Advaitaholics Anonymous* which rapidly gained a large readership amongst veteran spiritual seekers, many of whom had grown disillusioned after years of being mired in fruitless spiritual teachings. In his writings, they found a refreshingly honest, down-to-earth, no-nonsense approach to the existential questions of life. This book is a compilation of some of his selected essays and serves as testimony of a man who has found his own mind.

A Canadian citizen born and raised in India, Shiv has been living with his wife and two daughters in snowy Hokkaido, Japan's northernmost island, where he has been working as a Business Strategy consultant. He can be contacted through his Facebook page: *Advaitaholics Anonymous*

ADVAITAHOLICS ANONYMOUS

Sobering Insights for Spiritual Addicts

Shiv Sengupta

New Sarum Press
UNITED KINGDOM

ADVAITAHOLICS ANONYMOUS

First published by New Sarum Press October 2020

ISBN: 978-1-9162903-6-5

New Sarum Press

www.newsarumpress.com

https://advaitaholics.com

Contents

Author's note

In the late summer of 2018, I created a Facebook blog page on a whim and began writing articles which cast a sober yet satirical glance on contemporary spirituality and the culture that is woven around it. The page was called *Advaitaholics Anonymous* and within a very short time it won a strong support among many seasoned seekers; individuals who had followed various 'spiritual' teachers, read all the literature, practised various meditative techniques yet were left with the vacant feeling that in the end it had all been a form of escape.

The page also earned its fair share of critics. *Advaitaholics Anonymous* remained controversial from the first post to its very last. By the end,[1] the page had thousands of readers worldwide. Over the span of a year, a total of a hundred and ninety articles were featured on it; I have selected forty-nine of them to appear in this book.

To me, 'enlightenment' is not some pinnacle state of consciousness but rather is a continuous process of ever-increasing clarity about self and reality—one that every sentient being is engaged with whether one is aware of it or not.

1. *Advaitaholics Anonymous* has since started up again [www.facebook.com/Advaitaholics-Anonymous-471671813352841]. Also, the website: advaitaholics.com

INTRODUCTION

What *is* an Advaitaholic?

'Advaitaholic' is a term that I coined in reference to the phenomenon of spiritual addiction; an addiction that plagues so many seekers who claim to be in search of a higher truth, transcendence, awakening, enlightenment, liberation or whatever other form that holy grail may take. And although the term appears to single out *Advaita*[2] as its focus, it is much broader than that. It encompasses all forms of spiritual belief systems and doctrine.

Spirituality is a highly personal business. It is a person's unique relationship with reality. Yet, the moment it is taken out of the person and objectified in the form of a system of thought it is no longer a personal affair. Once it is made concrete for others to congregate and build a community or culture around then that spirituality—our own relationship with reality—ceases to be the focal point.

Most of what we call 'spirituality' today—the communes, the ashrams, the temples, the online communities, the philosophies, the institutions, the satsangs[3] and such—have very little to do with spirituality at all. They are distractions whose primary focus is to create a culture of identity—the feeling of belonging to a group. Spirituality simply becomes reduced to nothing more than a useful foundation around which to build and sustain that culture.

2. *Advaita*: from the Sanskrit 'not two'—the Eastern philosophy of non-duality.
3. *Satsang*: literally 'company of truth', more often understood as a gathering of spiritual seekers, often with focus on a teacher or specific spiritual teachings.

But this is not something unique to spirituality alone. Most cultures work in this way; ethnic cultures, political cultures, music cultures, fashion cultures. Culture exists to provide an individual with a socially sanctioned worldview and a corresponding sense of identity which then allows that person to be safely inserted somewhere within the hierarchical fold. And the standard price one pays in exchange for the existential security and sense of belonging culture provides is that *one token of truth* we were all born with—that is our very birthright.

What is especially ironic about spiritual culture is that it promises to return that token to us. The token we once naively traded away. But this is, of course, a lie. Because if that token were to be returned as promised, the culture itself would capitulate overnight. For who would remain to support it?

If all became liberated as the gurus promise, who would remain to follow them, to support them, to worship and idolize them? It comes as no surprise then that these same gurus appear to have a poor track record of actually 'liberating' those whom they claim to teach. Liberation was never the end goal here. Domestication was, by which I mean the acceptance of sociocultural fetters.

There are those who have arrived at this deflating realization the hard way. Now that they've exhausted every avenue that promised them salvation from suffering they find themselves at an impasse. Many are jaded, bitter, angry. And they wonder in their confusion:

> *Was I delusional even to question things in the first place? Was that impulse, to delve deeper into myself, that started me off on this journey—before the books, before the gurus, before the communities—was that impulse, that instinct, just a false hope?*

Through the insights in this book, I encourage you to revisit everything you think you know about yourself, about the world, about spirituality, about teachers and yet to trust in your own intuition, first and foremost. While the bathwater may be murky, there is still a baby somewhere in there.

In the end, spirituality is really about getting sober. Developing the courage to see life as it is, without needing to inflate it with escapist love and light rhetoric nor resorting to a nihilistic resignation by declaring that everything is just illusion and thus meaningless. Sobriety involves engaging with life in its all-encompassing ordinariness and taking responsibility for it in all its manifestations, the good, the bad and the ugly, not only for our own part. I mean taking full ownership of our circumstances, however they may appear. If I get hit by a car tomorrow from no fault of my own—then, even though I am not responsible for how it happened, I *am* responsible for how I choose to face the aftermath.

When common sense becomes the highest form of wisdom to which we can aspire, and sanity the greatest kind of enlightenment, then it is safe to say that the path of recovery has truly begun.

CHAPTER 1

GETTING SOBER

Let me be clear. This book isn't about Advaita. It is about addiction. And addiction relates to substance abuse.

That substance can take the form of a drink or a narcotic. It can take the form of an activity that we feel compelled to do even to our own detriment: like sex or work or exercise. And it can take the form of an ideology or belief system and the culture surrounding it: like religion, communism or scientism.

The substance itself is often neither harmful nor beneficial. It may be designed to produce a certain effect within the individual. The addiction is the issue. And one can become addicted to pretty much anything one can imagine: a car, a person, a pet, a hobby, a lifestyle, a habit, a group, a job...

Addiction restructures the reality we perceive and arranges it according to its own agenda. It hijacks the basic intelligence of the body and brain and allows them to operate only in accordance with its own perspectives. The body and brain comply and are stimulated by this process which hijacks their 'natural' mode of expression.

Addiction is an internal Stockholm Syndrome[4] whereby our substance of choice holds us captive and refuses to release us. In the process we fall in love with our captor and rationalize its actions as beneficial.

No matter what kind of addiction we might have, this is the dynamic. An irrational love for the substance,[5] even in the face

4. Stockholm Syndrome: the name for a condition where hostages start to develop strong emotional bonds with their captors.

5. In the case of process addictions such as gambling or sex, the

of abuse, often accompanied by a sense of self-loathing.

The substance can be anything: a liquor, a narcotic, a person, an ideology.

In truth, most of us are addicts in some way or another, to some degree. This is because a sense of lack is almost universal within human beings. And it seems that the journey for most people is about how to resolve that feeling of lack. While part of this feeling of lack may be conscious, most of it is unconscious. The void we feel inside goes deep.

What we call 'life' becomes nothing more than a series of strategies to fill that void.

Some believe that material objects will somehow satisfy that lack. So, they are driven by a need to acquire a vast amount of money, assets, homes, businesses and so on.

Some believe that emotional experiences will fill that lack. So, they are driven by a need to find the ideal partner, start a family, maintain a large circle of friends, acquaintances, social networks and so on.

Others believe that theories and concepts will fill that lack. So, they are driven by a need to acquire knowledge, build systems of thought, beliefs or ideology.

Still others believe that having spiritual or mystical experiences will fill that lack. So, they are driven by a need to attain altered states of consciousness, peak experiences and mystical union.

No one seeks in purely one direction. Most people are simultaneously seeking in more than one of these arenas of life, but there is always one area that is dominant when compared to the rest. And that is what informs the construction of our primary identity.

The holy grail is the one-size-fits-all solution that will perfectly resolve that sense of void. And that holy grail may take

'substance' may be the individual's own neurohormones, such as dopamine or oxytocin, production of which is triggered by certain activities or processes.

the form of extreme wealth, the perfect love, a unified theory of everything or spiritual enlightenment.

Yet, the hour of disillusionment is inevitable. It is the moment when we realize that no matter how much we accumulate in the substance of our choice, it can never fill the void for long. The sense of lack is always lurking in the background. That void is a bottomless pit.

Rather than fully facing up to this fact, many people will simply change their seeking strategy.

If acquiring material wealth did not satisfy, perhaps starting a family will. If that doesn't eventually satisfy, then perhaps embarking on a spiritual path will. Same holy grail, different form.

When every avenue has been thoroughly exhausted we always end up back where we started. In the midst of a void that cannot be filled....

I was speaking to someone yesterday, who has arrived at exactly this point. He told me how realizing that no external object nor internal experience will ever satisfy, he finds himself at an impasse. He has exhausted all his avenues. He has seen that they are all dead ends, including the spiritual path. Yet still, what he calls the *Truth* eludes him.

He holds on to this notion of the Truth that he feels is beyond him. He has arrived at the conclusion that perhaps it is just too complex for him to grasp. That he should probably make his peace with the fact that he may never get it.

I suggested that the case is quite different: Truth is the most obvious and evident thing there is. And it is so simple it can't be grasped by an idea. To seek it is to miss it, because seeking makes one look away from it.

Truth is simply what you are looking at. Call it *life, the universe and everything,*[6] none of these words can do it justice. It's

6. Adams, Douglas. 2016. *The Hitchiker's Guide to the Galaxy.* Pan, London.

much more obvious than these words imply.

Look around, I said. *Look what's in front of your nose. Has this ever not been there? Don't try to say or define what it is. Just look at it. It's always present.*

But how about what's looking? he asks. *That feels different. What about the internal life?*

Look at that too. What's behind your nose? That has also always been present. You could call it a 'self' or a 'me' or a 'Shiv' or 'awareness' or whatever. But none of those words do it justice.

But it feels 'separate' from what I'm looking at, he says.

It is separate. In its form. In the way it appears. In the substance it seems to be made of. But notice something else. The two always exist together.

What is in front of your nose can't exist without what is behind your nose. The two realities arise together and recede together, they ebb and flow as one even if they appear entirely different. Like the heads and tails of a spinning coin...

Truth is the whole of it. Always right here. Always obvious.

The 'void' is what we create through the force of our denial of the truth that is always staring us in the face. And every attempt to fill the void is really a reinforcement of that denial. It is a refusal to accept what is real and present, by envisioning an 'alternative truth', an ideal reality in which no such void exists.

Hence, the irony, that it is the alternative truth that creates the void. The void is the chasm between the truth and its alternative. Between what is and what could be.

Which is why facing the void and then sitting smack in the middle of it is the only reasonable thing to do. It is usually the last resort that people arrive at when there is nowhere left to go. And as unbearable as it feels for a time, the very act of sitting and being present with it is how it transforms.

As the pull towards an alternative reality gradually loses its hold, the reality surrounding us comes to the fore, gradually becoming the only benchmark of experience. And the truth that is inherent in its presence becomes increasingly more evident.

This is what the process of getting sober looks like no matter what the addiction:

It begins with a firm willingness to sit with the void, a refusal to succumb to the substance of addiction, a long period of withdrawal animated by acute suffering, a newfound sense of clarity that comes with sobriety, a period of disorientation and readjustment to daily life.

It is in this final stage that many who become sober eventually relapse because they are yet to fully become grounded in their sobriety. It still feels too unfamiliar. This book acts as a resource for such people.

Getting sober is a tough road in itself. But it's in *staying* sober that the mechanism of addiction eventually dissolves.

CHAPTER 2

ON THE EDGE OF ENLIGHTENMENT

Q: Sometimes when I sit in meditation for long enough, relax enough/let go enough/surrender enough (or whatever words you want to use) I get to a point where I'm scared to let go any more. If I let go any further, I will be consumed by something unknown. It freaks me out and I can't help but stop. It's almost like letting go is the same as dying.

This isn't some *die before you die* spiritual bullshit that I read somewhere. It really feels like a point of no return of some sort. But that's ridiculous—what could possibly happen? I'm sitting on my couch for fuck's sake! And yet it feels terminal. Like something could go seriously wrong if I continue. Any thoughts?

A: I remember sitting under a tree at Queen's Park in Toronto years ago feeling exactly what you are feeling now. And man! How close I felt to that edge! I was dangling from a precipice over an abyss holding on for dear life with just the edges of my fingertips! I felt terrified to let go. But I knew that it was just a matter of time before I either let go willingly or my grip slipped. And the panic that gripped me was paralyzing. I was frightened beyond belief!

And then one day the unthinkable happened...

I realized that I was just playing games with myself in my head.

And I can tell you now that it *is* all a game. The holding on, the letting go, the fear of what will happen, the desire to surrender, the feeling of dying and never coming back, the confusion, the desperation—it's all mind games.

You are desperately attempting to get ahead of yourself. To win some unwinnable match against yourself that exists only in your imagination. You may deny it and say that this isn't what you are doing. But it's happening, whether you are aware of it or not. You are spinning at a furious pace attempting to catch your own tail. And sure, you might end up feeling dizzy and disoriented at the end of all that spinning. You may even see some stars. But that is nothing to write home about.

All these words we use: *holding on, surrender, ego, awareness, asleep, awake*. What meaning do they have? They help our minds make sense of life, but they are *not* life itself. Just as the words *east, west, north* and *south* may help us orient ourselves on the globe but they are arbitrary terms we created. The planet has no fixed cardinal directions.

Every experience you speak about can only have meaning in relation to another experience you've already had. This experience that you are having right now only feels extraordinary or significant because it is different in comparison to how you are used to feeling.

What *is* letting go, exactly? It can only be defined in relation to holding on. Then what is holding on?

Everything is defined in terms of something else in an endless web of ideas about what is/could/should be happening.

None of this has any relevance to life itself. Awareness is always present and undiminished, regardless of the shape or form your personal experience may take. It's not as if surrendering makes me any more aware than holding on. The same person in the same situation could suddenly see things in a whole new light. It's just that the contents of awareness stay the same. When you find that your overhead cabin luggage has shifted at the end of a flight because of turbulence it's just a matter of, *So what—big deal!* It's still the same plane, same contents, same passengers, same everything. All that has shifted is the position of things. Other than that, nothing has really changed. Similarly, all that may shift is our perspective, but these shifts are just a natural outcome of living a life. Every human being on this planet experiences shifts in perspectives. Certain events have a tendency to shift our outlook more drastically—injury, death of a loved one, divorce, the sudden end of a career, loss of finances and certain spiritual revelations. But in the end nothing about reality is any different. It's just that you are now seeing it from a slightly different angle.

That reorientation, whether sudden or gradual, happens to all of us, some time in our life, regardless of how spiritually or otherwise oriented we may be. In fact, rather than reaching for an elevated perspective on life, the most sensible thing you can do is remain open to life as it comes. Rather than trying to get an advantage, enjoy the freedom to view life as it is. Rather than trying to get the inside track on this whole reality deal, staying open to life as it happens allows for a person to occupy multiple angles on reality. It gives you the freedom to view life from different viewpoints.

By remaining 'open' to life, I mean by not fixating on one particular experience. Because the moment we fixate, awareness narrows its attention down into a tunnel vision that focuses on that experience at the expense of everything else happening around us. Hyper-focusing on that inside track, we lose sight of the whole road.

And even if, arguably, you were to get onto that inside track —even if you got to the end of the racetrack—then what? What has changed other than the fact that you now see from a different perspective than you did? Even if you become like the next Ramana Maharshi[7] or Buddha, is this something to celebrate? What has really changed? Take a look at the trees and ask them

7. Ramana Maharshi: 1879-1950 CE. Indian sage, teacher of Advaita Vedanta and 'self-inquiry': www.sriramanamaharshi.org

if they give a fuck for how enlightened you've become.

There may be humans, people who do give a fuck. But then people seem to give a fuck about a lot of things that are not worth giving a fuck about. A whole lot of people seem to really care what Kanye West[8] has to say about politics. So what? What has really changed about anything other than the fact that some people now look at you a bit differently?

It's all games in the mind. And what we call 'spirituality' and the whole guru world is just those same mind games played out on a bigger scale. If you're playing imaginary tea party with your dolls in your house and I'm playing imaginary tea party with my dolls in my house, then hell! we can play imaginary tea party together! And if we get enough folks together who want to play imaginary tea party then we can have events, conferences, galas and getaways where all everyone ever does is play imaginary tea party.

Nothing wrong with imaginary tea parties. Nothing wrong with enlightenment games. As long as those involved all know it's a game. The moment it becomes real, then this planet turns into an asylum.

Here's a reality check. Whether you surrender or not makes not one ounce of difference to anything. You're still going to get old. You're still going to get sick. You're still going to have some days that you quietly wish were better and others that you feel are perfect the way they are. You're still going to have to pay bills and swear the government is trying to stiff you. And eventually you're going to die.

And maybe some people will remember certain profound words you once said. And maybe they will speak highly of you. And maybe they will have book clubs or 'Spirituality Sundays' where they get together over coffee and muffins to talk about some of your deep and meaningful utterings. But, truthfully

8. Kanye West: b. 1977 CE. Musician, fashion designer, practicing Christian. Popular in the first half of 21st century CE.

speaking, they won't really be giving a fuck about you. It's themselves they will really be giving a fuck about.

So, on that cheerful note, keep doing what you are doing. Or not. You asked me for my thoughts and here they are. But if I can leave you with one final bit of counsel...

It's quite common in spiritual literature to tell someone to listen to that 'still small voice within'. And that sort of advice has its place depending on what a person is experiencing. But in your case, that still small voice sounds more like a deafening scream to me. And if you are uncertain which voice it is that I'm talking about, it's the one that's saying:

'I'm sitting on my couch for fuck's sake!'

CHAPTER 3
WHERE ALL PATHS LEAD

Here is the biggest mistake in spirituality, one that almost every seeker inadvertently makes—which is to believe that *the goal of spiritual practice is to transcend suffering.* Spiritual practices *cannot* help people transcend suffering. When people engage in spiritual practice with the goal of transcending suffering, *that* is their biggest error.

Whether we're repenting for our sins, striving to break the karmic cycle of rebirth, attempting to transcend the ego or whatever other flavor our spiritual endeavors may take on, in the end the motivation is always the same: to break free of the limitations and constraints we live within that cause us to suffer.

We are driven by a deep discontent and resistance towards our lot in life, however that may be manifesting. Whatever it is that plagues us: uncertainty, grief, fear, insecurity, rage, yearning, loneliness, disgust, terror or trauma—spirituality then becomes the path that promises a way out. A solution to the problem of existence.

I can't blame anyone for thinking this way. After all, pretty much every religion or wisdom path that we have encountered has pushed forward this view. Salvation from sin for the Christian, freedom from bondage for the Buddhist, breaking the karmic cycle of rebirth and suffering for the Hindu, dissociating altogether from the problems the 'little me' suffers by claiming no-selfhood and no-doership for the Neo-Advaitist. The hook is always the promise of escape.

All paths lead to the truth is a saying often used to validate different spiritual approaches. I see it differently: *all paths lead away from the truth,* because they draw us away from whatever it is we are experiencing in the moment towards something that we feel, or are told, we *ought* to be experiencing.

We are forever subverting life as it is happening right now for a version that we'd rather have happen. In fact, this sort of approach forms the basis of pretty much any spiritual practice. What makes us actually believe that sitting for an hour of meditation is any more relevant to our spirituality than eating an ice cream cone? Or that serving free meals at the temple is more spiritually meritorious than getting into a spat with the missus?

These 'practices' we engage in have absolutely nothing to do with spirituality. Praying five times a day may make a man much more religious than the sex worker, but it doesn't make him any more spiritual. There are no degrees, quantities or hierarchies within spirituality.

Spiritual practice is not something that we need to try and contrive. It is something that is happening by nature of the fact that we are alive. A spiritual being has no choice but to engage in spiritual practice. Life is the ultimate spiritual practice. It is the *only* spiritual practice. Everything else is rites and rituals; traditional and cultural exercises whose impact on our spiritual experience is much the same as the causative input of a sneeze on a *tsunami*.

And so, if life *is* spiritual practice and the experience of suffering is a big part of life, then how can the goal of spiritual practice be to transcend it? That's like saying the goal of a runner is to stop running, or the goal of a rock climber is to stop climbing. Suffering is a fundamental part of the experience of living because suffering forms the context of the practice. It provides the terrain: complete with obstacles, gradients, impassable patches and detours which we navigate and so develop our skill.

A climber who looks at the mountain as an obstacle to be avoided has completely missed the point of his or her sport. A runner who views the road as an inconvenience is misguided about the purpose of running.

Then how can it be any different for the seeker who seeks to transcend their suffering?

The suffering *is* the context within which our practice happens. All the pain, the misery, the fear, the uncertainty, the rage, the disgust, the terror and trauma *is* what spiritual practice looks like. I'm not talking about what they advertise on the brochures.

Give me a hemorrhoid pillow over a meditation pillow any day, is what I say.

But who wants to believe this? Who wants to believe that experiencing the soul-crushing boredom of the boardroom is spiritual practice? (And I don't mean *turning it into* a meditation! But just actually being bored out of your wits.) Who wants to believe that letting out those gut-wrenching sobs over the body of a loved one is spiritual practice? Who wants to believe that experiencing impotent anger and flipping the middle finger at the driver who just cut you off is spiritual practice? Who wants to believe that the feeling of sheer panic that grips you, as your mind convinces you that everyone on the train must certainly be staring at you and judging you, is spiritual practice? Who wants to believe the butterflies you feel in your stomach when *he* walks into the room and the rush of jealousy you feel in your body as he smiles at someone else is spiritual practice?

Life presents us with unique spiritual exercises of varying degrees of challenge, from moment to moment, in the form of our everyday experiences, and yet we convince ourselves that sitting on a cushion and staring off into space is somehow the most superior option available to us.

This is what happens when human beings trade in their own innate intelligence for the dull, stale, flat and unprofitable logic of groupthink. No! Forget the fact that this body you possess is one of a kind, this brain you possess is one of a kind, the experiences of your life are one of a kind, the pain you have suffered is one of a kind, your frustration and despair are one of a kind. Forget that what stirs your blood and floats your boat is one of a kind. Forget all that! Let's all sit the same way, face the same way, adopt the same dull facial expressions, the same unearthly tones in our voices and try to escape everything about us that is utterly unique. Monkey see, monkey do. Evolution, it seems, is moving backwards.

Spirituality, as it is widely practiced, is simply the process of lobotomizing yourself.

All paths lead away from the truth because why else would a person take that path unless we believed that the goal were somewhere other than right where we're at? By placing the goal outside ourselves, in a place other than here, in a time other than now, in the form of an action other than the one that is already taking place—these so-called 'spiritual paths' present us with nothing more than life-negating strategies. They are designed to actively subvert the immediacy of actual experience, regardless of how it may appear, with some empty promise of a better moment to come. Dethrone the true king and place the scheming vizier on the throne.

By scapegoating suffering and making transcending it our active goal, these paths strip the climber of the very mountain she loves to climb, the runner of the very road he loves to run on. It strips a person of the very marrow of spiritual experience.

The most significant realization I have ever had was that suffering is endless. This is not something to despair about. But it is something to absolutely rejoice in. It's like telling a runner that he will never run out of roads to run. Or a climber that she will never run out of mountains to climb. But, in that simple shift in perspective, suffering itself transforms from something terrifying into something inspiring.

It ceases to be the boogeyman lurking in the shadows. It becomes our muse.

CHAPTER 4

AMBIVALENCE

Q: How does one function in any meaningful way in this world without beliefs? I'm afraid: will I become an ambivalent or apathetic person? Isn't 'not believing' a kind of spiritual bypassing? [9]

A. This question strikes right at the heart of the seeker's dilemma.

We're convinced that without beliefs we'll either turn into ravenous barbarians who wouldn't hesitate to devour each other the first chance we get. Or we'll become these emotionally detached ascended masters gazing down upon humanity from our Himalayan caves as far away from the madness as possible. The first case is clearly abhorrent to most and the second may have a niche appeal but for many feels like a cop out.

So, let's begin with a reality check.

Firstly, we don't need to lose belief in order to turn into ravenous barbarians. Belief systems do an excellent job of supporting that sort of behavior. One need only glance into history to see how we have behaved in truly despicable ways (far worse than our animal cousins) in order to uphold our beliefs. It is a myth that civilization has brought us out of barbarism. Civilization has only turned us into more sophisticated barbarians. Whereas before you'd have to don war paint and hack your enemies down with an ax one by one, now you can simply operate a drone to wipe out an entire village thousands of miles away while still in your underwear.

---

9. Definition of spiritual bypassing can be found at: Welwood, J. 2000. *Toward a Psychology of Awakening.* Boston, MA: Shambhala Publications.

Secondly, life in a Himalayan cave is tough. Think about it. We are talking about a cold and barren wasteland where barely anything grows. Unless you are a mountaineer or have grown up in those sorts of harsh climes the urge to opt for that sort of radical change of address really has no rational basis. These romantic images we conjure up of sages in the mountains are really remnants of certain ascetic cultures that have always been driven by a philosophy of radical deprivation in order to realize the self. We see them in all religions. But radical deprivation is not what we are talking about here.

Still, I can see why many of us are unnerved at the thought of losing our beliefs. The spiritual circus and its centre stage performers have done nothing to ground our views of what such a reality looks like. If we are drenched in Universal Love then how can we continue to honor our familial bonds? Wouldn't that be showing preferential treatment? If we have realized the self to be unreal, how can we continue to act in a manner that benefits that self? How can we take care of our own needs?

These are the sorts of pseudo-dilemmas that plague us, steeped as we are in magical thinking and wildly romantic views of what a sane and awakened existence looks like.

It's easy to revere that Indian sage clad only in a loincloth, reclining like an artists' model on his daybed, his bare chest a testament to his rejection of norms of presentability while being fed rice and sambar by the loving hands of his devotees. And yet, no one in their right mind really wants to end up like that.

Living without beliefs is not spiritual bypassing

Let's start with the last part of the question.

What we term 'spiritual bypassing' is not really the same as living without beliefs. In fact, spiritual bypassing is just the adoption of a different set of beliefs that promote an attitude of self-escape.

And everyone's doing it. This is not just a phenomenon unique to spiritual culture. It's a very human experience. In fact, the word 'spiritual' in the term 'spiritual bypassing' is a misleading one, which is why I would rather eschew this term. Something like 'existential bypassing' is more inclusive. It encompasses all aspects of our lives.

Every political ideology we adopt, every religious doctrine we believe in, every social narrative we buy into, every corporate agenda we fall prey to is a form of existential bypassing. You are bypassing your immediate reality in favor of an idealized one. That is what a bypass is. It's a path that allows one to avoid the main road: to skirt around the issue.

And in that sense, belief is a bypassing strategy. Not the other way around. The moment we adopt any sort of belief whether it be a spiritual one or otherwise, we are constructing an alternate route by which to traverse this reality: a kind of detour or shortcut. And while that alternative route may not have been constructed solely for the purpose of escape, merely the fact that it exists makes escape a tempting choice that most will take any chance they get. When stuck in a traffic jam it's human nature to want to take an alternate route if one exists, rather than just staying put without progressing.

So, when we are operating from a point of minimal belief, one is essentially locked into this ground zero reality as it exists. There is no real desire to get off the highway because:

a. There are not many different routes to choose from.

b. There is nowhere to progress to.

The highway is endless and we remain on it until we don't. So, the only logical option is to sit back and enjoy the ride.

Ambivalence is not apathy

We turn now to the second part of the question.

Many assume that an ambivalent position on the pressing issues of life and society implies a kind of apathy. But ambivalence is really a mature perspective through which we no longer see things existing in contrast to other things.

Nothing in life is ever black and white. Everything sustains everything else, no matter how opposed they appear to be. No phenomenon occurs in isolation but rather causes, and is caused by, everything else that exists. When presented with such an intricate web, ambivalence is the only reasonable response; it is really an admission of our own limitations at grasping the whole picture.

Further, the ambivalent approach promotes an aesthetic experience of reality that is lacking in the binary approach. A photographer understands that the beauty of a photograph lies in the balance of contrast: that too much light overexposes and too much darkness makes the image murky. Similarly, one understands that the forces of light and darkness in humanity are neither good nor bad but rather create something akin to art, if and when they manifest in a delicate balance with one another. This aesthetic approach doesn't seek to banish the shadows in favor of the light but seeks to bring them together in balance within our own mind.

There are primal forces far more ancient than us that continue to operate through us and every other creation in this universe. There is a fundamental duality that forms the basis of all experience. And every phenomenon that has ever occurred in the history of the universe is the result of an interaction of those dual forces. Human society is no exception. And all our progress as a civilization has resulted from the interaction of those forces. There can be no eliminating one in favor of the other.

Ambivalence[10] is not the same as apathy. The word 'apathy' derives from the Greek word, *apathes* (*a* = without; *pathos* = suffering/feeling). The binary viewpoint, in that vein, reveals itself as the truly apathetic one. Because it lacks the aesthetic basis from which life can truly be 'felt' and appreciated for what it is. In taking a one-sided approach, it ruthlessly carves reality into two halves which remain alienated from one another forever.

Functioning in a meaningful way

Finally, the first question. How do we function in a meaningful way if we don't believe?

For example, how do we build careers or start families, sustain relationships, stand up against injustices and so on if we don't have some sort of a belief as the basis of how we must act?

We don't need beliefs in order to function. Every other organism on the planet seems to do just fine. By functioning in a 'meaningful' way I take this to mean that we can come to terms with our participation in the human drama, even if we have seen through the fiction of it.

Fortunately for us, our brains come equipped with this nifty app that we all use quite often. It's called the *Willing Suspension of Disbelief.*[11]

In order to function in human society, it's not belief that we need but rather the ability to suspend 'disbelief'. Now, I'm not artfully playing with words here. This is a very real phenomenon.

Why do we enjoy films, novels, video-games and theater so much? Clearly, when we see Tom Cruise catapulting himself off a skyscraper onto a soaring helicopter, we don't believe it's real.

---

10. Ambivalence: from the Latin *ambi* = in two ways and *valere* = to be strong.

11. A term coined by the English poet, Samuel Taylor Coleridge (1772-1834) and explored earlier by the ancient Greek Philosopher, Aristotle.

Or when tears roll down our cheeks as the guy proposes to the girl in the middle of a crowded airport just before she's about to board her flight to obscurity. We don't actually believe that happened, but still the tears come. Or when the shadow of the velociraptor appears on the bedroom walls, we don't actually believe dinosaurs still exist. And yet, we are able to experience those moments with our full range of emotions precisely because, in that moment, we don't disbelieve them either. We have made the choice willingly to suspend our disbelief in order to be entertained by an alternate reality. One that allows us to love, hate, be euphoric, be enraged, be inspired, be horrified, be disgusted, be aroused while knowing full well that that reality is only a fictional overlay.

Everyone knows what it's like sitting next to that know-it-all in the theater who guffaws at the sentimental scenes and criticizes the factual basis of the film right when the historic battle between the hero and his nemesis is unfolding. We call that person a spoilsport. And in that sense, any guru (who is not faking it) who proposes a rejection of this human drama is just being a spoilsport. To which I generally respond—*You are at the theater: shut it, grab a bag of popcorn and enjoy the fun*.

To be without beliefs does not imply that we no longer feel motivated at work, or invested in our families or horrified by atrocities in society and so on. In fact, when we are able to live in that narrow window of perception between belief and disbelief, it frees us up to experience life in so many different flavors.

In the absence of belief, we are no longer gun-shy about fully expressing ourselves and experiencing the themes and genres we are truly interested in, rather than the ones prescribed to us. Yet, with the suspension of disbelief, nor do we want to gripe and moan about how stupid this human reality is and walk out of the theater.

Shakespeare's words[12] ring true to our experience of the

12. 'All the world's a stage, And all the men and women merely players'

world being a stage and us being the players. To take the drama as real would be a sort of insanity and yet to storm off the stage would be merely petulant.

The only mature response here is to do the best damn job of playing our part that we can manage.

Until the curtain falls.

— *As You Like It* (Act II, Scene VII).

Chapter 5
THE REUNION

The cold wind howled, viciously rattling the windows every now and then, like a spectre in chains. In the dim starlight, the rugged Himalayan peaks rose like the gnarly spiked back of some prehistoric behemoth. The residents in the small mountain village of Gulmarg were all sheltered safely indoors. From my bedroom in the attic, I could hear faint laughter from the living room as my parents and their friends drank pints of ale and feasted on legs of curried mutton.

I turned off the oil lamp next to my bed and stared up at the sloped ceiling. In the corner of the room, the Bukhari, a traditional Kashmiri wood-burning stove, crackled and spat giving off a warm enveloping heat that made my eyelids droop. Still, I fought off sleep because I hadn't yet performed my nightly ritual.

This ritual was a game of dare that I would play with what I called 'the Silence'. Every night as I lay in bed, I'd allow the quietness of the room to become the focus of my attention. At first, it would be barely noticeable. But as I continued to focus on it, the Silence would grow in what I can only describe as 'heard sound', moving from a whisper, to a clear hum and finally to a deafening roar of static in my ears. And, then... Inevitably, there would come a point when the Silence would feel so overwhelming and so menacing that I would become scared and shift my attention to something else. And in that moment the Silence would subside. Each night I would push the envelope just a bit further.

But beyond just the experience of being with the Silence,

there was something else that was very apparent to my six-year-old self. And that was that the Silence was not some inanimate thing. It was not merely some sensory experience. Whether the result of a child's vivid imagination or the perception of something beyond what we as adults can see: the Silence felt like a living entity to me. In fact, I perceived it as a being something like a god, although I didn't think of it as that at the time. 'God'—in my childhood mind—was a pantheon of deities with multiple arms, multiple superpowers and multiple support animals, not unlike the *Justice League*.[13] God was something you made stories about.

Yet, the Silence was something real, something living. And it knew me in a way that I didn't know myself. Which is why it was always present, always watching, always lurking, waiting for a moment when I might drop my guard, and then it would show itself. I was both terrified and mystified by it. And when it appeared, I would experience this inner push-pull sensation with one part of me wanting to move towards it and another to get the hell away from it.

I didn't believe it was evil, nor did I believe it was good. What I did feel, however, was that it was something ancient, infinitely older than the Himalayas themselves. And there was something in me that suspected I already knew the Silence but simply couldn't remember. Perhaps, I had come from it, this pulsing living womb of creation. And if I had been created from it, then that is where I would be destroyed. That is why I feared it. I suspected, deep down, that to fully embrace it would mean to be annihilated by it.

Though I performed the ritual over many nights, I never went all the way in. Eventually, I just stopped playing. And after a while, the Silence simply stopped visiting.

***

13. www.dccomics.com/characters/justice-league.

Fifteen years later, I found myself seated at the edge of a pier along the coast of Lake Ontario, Canada. This version of what I still called 'me' was someone different entirely. The six-year-old had been a child of great energy, enthusiasm, courage and excitement for life, yet, the ensuing fifteen years would wither his spirit, hollow out his heart and turn his mind into a dungeon of deranged voices. More than anything I wanted release from the torment that had become my life. Even the courage I had once possessed had evaporated. I was a coward, pathetic and unable to muster up enough energy to even put an end to myself.

My family felt helpless to address the circumstance. I was put on anti-depressants—one dose was all I took. I isolated myself and sank into a depression that lasted for years and deepened further by the day.

The day on the pier, I had been practically dragged out of the house by my father and sister for a ferry ride to one of Toronto's islands. Having arrived there, however, I wanted nothing to do with the 'fun activities' the two of them had planned so I left them and sauntered off on my own. When I arrived at the pier there was something mythical about it. It seemed like the final stop. The end of the road before solid ground gave way to a vast blue nothing that stretched to the horizon. Perhaps, it was this symbolism that drew me onto that pier and all the way towards its edge.

I sat down on a bench and gazed out at the lake—blue, empty, still. I felt utterly spent. And knew that this was my final resting place. After this I wouldn't have the energy to do one more thing. As I looked out over the water, I heard a familiar whisper. Something stirred in a dusty corner of my memory as my attention focused in on it. It was like meeting an old forgotten friend—the Silence came visiting again.

This time there wasn't any fear or resistance within me. All of that had been spent. There wasn't an ounce of courage left within me to fight or pull back. I didn't even have the energy to feel terrified. I was numb, dead already. A corpse in living flesh. And so, when the Silence came, it came unimpeded. I watched helplessly as my being was drawn past its event horizon, before it enveloped me and then infiltrated me: my body, my mind. In some bizarre process of spiritual transfusion every ounce of what I considered to be 'me' was replaced with Silence.

Over the next four months, I walked around in a waking daze. My mind, my thoughts, my self-identity had been hijacked and replaced with the perspective of Silence. I was now seeing through *it's* eyes. Seeing the world the way *it* saw. I was no longer myself. I *was* the Silence.

And the world it revealed was something entirely different: vibrant, alive, intricately connected, inseparably one. It took over my consciousness by shutting off my parasitic mind. And in the process, my hollowed heart began to heal again and my withered spirit began to resuscitate.

Then one day, the Silence started to fade. It moved out slowly. Over a period of weeks. And as it did, several systems in my brain began coming back online. Thoughts began operating more fluidly again. My familiar sense of self began to return. And as this happened, I held on to the silence for dear life.

I didn't want to go back to being me! I wanted the Silence to stay for good. And still it faded, but always remained in the background as a barely audible hum, available for me to reach anytime I felt the urge.

The mind I was left with was similar in many ways to the one I'd had: my personality had been left intact, yet many aspects of my thinking had been rewired. I found I was unable to feel such intense amounts of misery or self-loathing again. I was unable to have suicidal thoughts again. I was unable to sink into that depth of depression again.

Still, there were several things that hadn't changed. None of my dilemmas, my existential confusions, my sense of purpose or lack thereof had been solved for me. None of my past traumas had been resolved. That work, the Silence had left unfinished. All the Silence had done for me was revitalize my spirit, my resolve and my love for life by showing me what reality looked like from its perspective.

***

Seven years later, I found myself in a place of great confusion precipitated by the end of a relationship that I had poured my heart and soul into. Abruptly abandoned and left out on a limb, I felt lost, listless and terribly alone. And the gnawing void I'd always carried inside me, which I had attempted to fill with friends, spirituality, work and relationships, now became an inescapable reality of my day to day experience. The breakup sealed that fate and everything I had in my life suddenly lost meaning.

And so, I decided that, since the void was unavoidable, I would have to face it. The hole in myself, which I had walked around with for my entire life, was something that I couldn't turn away from anymore or attempt to fill up with some relationship or career pursuit. If it was a part of me then I wanted to get to know it.

Previously, I'd always lived with roommates. Instead, I found an apartment and furnished it minimally: nothing more than a sofa, a bed and a dresser for my clothes. I didn't have a TV, a computer, an internet connection, I didn't listen to music or even read any books. I turned my phone off when I entered the apartment and only turned it back on when I left for work in the mornings. Any object that could be used to fill up time I avoided. Every evening after returning from work, I'd sit on my balcony and gaze at the tops of trees and buildings across the city. Watching the trees sway in the breeze was the extent of entertainment I allowed myself.

Sitting there, I wasn't meditating in any formal way. There

was no real intention to my being there. I just sat with the hole —that void inside me. And I would listen to the Silence. It was always there. Sitting right beside me. Wordlessly encouraging me on.

Those hours spent on the balcony with that feeling of emptiness inside me were excruciating. At first it was terrifying, then miserable, then incredibly frustrating until eventually it just became dead boring. The only comfort I had through it all, was the Silence. And knowing it was with me no matter what.

Eventually, the dynamic changed. I don't remember when it happened. But I began to look forward to coming home and sitting with what I had come to call the 'hole'. Except it didn't feel like a hole anymore. It felt more like a 'whole'. Without any real intellectual understanding or rationalizing. Just on a dynamic and deeply felt visceral level.

And the Silence was no longer beside me. It was within me now. It had seeped in noiselessly, undetected by me, and had filled that entire void. Yet, this time 'I' was still present. My mind, my thoughts, my reason, my personality hadn't been overridden or replaced.

And for the first time I understood what the 'Silence' was, what the 'void' was, what this 'journey' had been.

The Silence was a deep and original aspect of myself that had been cut out of me long before I can remember. And the empty space that had been left behind was that 'hole', the void, I had always carried around.

The 'journey' had been one of reunion of self with self. It had been the integration of all that had been 'silenced' and shadowed: both dark and divine, back into my identity.

***

Spiritual literature often references silence as a path of spiritual practice. We tend to think of silence as an experience or process by which our minds learn to become quiet and calm. Yet, in my experience, it has been so much more than that. It is an aspect of who I am, of my identity, just as much as my own name, my own mind or personality. In its absence, my mind and personality grew unchecked and chaotic; now there is a balance between the form and formless within me. My mind is tempered by it and thus able to flourish in a healthy, organic fashion.

And my identity has evolved from merely being the form in which I appear: as my person, my thoughts, my emotions and my personality. Now, I am equally that formless Silence and the vibrant space it occupies.

Chapter 6
SQUARE ONE

This needs to be said…

The awakened perspective is just another perspective on life. No more valuable, no more significant, no more extraordinary than any other.

The value we perceive in anything—whether that be wealth, fame, love, success, power, happiness, excellence, genius or enlightenment—is generated by the experience of a very specific kind of fundamental lack that skews our perception of reality in such a way that it then orders reality into a hierarchy of experience. The pinnacle of that hierarchy is that one thing which most acutely addresses the feeling of lack and promises to fulfill it in the most comprehensive way.

But even though life contains these hierarchies—biological, psychological and social—life in itself is not hierarchical. It just *is.* I am no more alive than a flower, a bee or a reptile. I am no more alive than a banker, a junkie or a president. Whether I am awake and aware or just a hopelessly conditioned person is of absolutely no real consequence to reality itself. It is only of consequence to me and perhaps those with whom I come into contact. But in truth all I am is just another lens of perception. Whether the aperture of that lens is wide open to allow in as much of the view unfiltered as possible, or narrowed down to the most myopic of perspectives, doesn't affect the view one bit.

Why do we want to be awakened? Why do we want to perceive reality with greater clarity? Because we are biased. Make no mistake about that. We are biased because we *do* perceive life and reality in hierarchical terms. We are driven by the fundamental lack which manifests within us as an existential *angst*—a peculiar nameless brand of suffering that no amount of wealth, power, love, success, genius and so on can fulfill. So, we build this stacked model of reality in which the suffering self occupies the lowest rung and the awakened self occupies the highest.

Yet, awakening itself reveals that there are no rungs. Being awakened is not really anything more significant than being unawakened or anything else for that matter. It is experientially different, of course. But reality is the sum total of all experiences and doesn't restrict or make preferences for any particular set. In short, life just couldn't care less.

The awakened perspective is possibly the only one that attempts to align the personal view with that of the whole so thoroughly. It is the only one that is not attempting to manipulate its own perspectives in order to skew its self-significance. Rather it actively seeks to subvert its own agenda in order to align with the flow of the overall process. Yet, the moment we do that we must realize that even such an alignment is of no real consequence. Aligning with—or opposing—reality are two sides of the same coin. Flowing with the river or opposing the current changes the river's course not in the least.

No form of existence and no level of consciousness is any more significant than any other. There is no hierarchy. Life is a flat surface. The depths and pinnacles we perceive are really alternative horizontal options spread out over a level playing field. Evolution is nothing more than the lateral career move consciousness makes into another set of equally valid experiences.

Speaking from my own experience, upon reflecting on my life I see that nothing has fundamentally changed.

I once suffered profoundly, now I don't.

> I once saw myself in very limited and predictable terms, now I don't.
>
> I once cared what other people thought about me, now I don't.
>
> I once placed my source of happiness, peace and fulfillment outside myself, now I don't.
>
> I once saw this experience of life as a hostile one, now I don't.
>
> I once held many beliefs about reality, now I don't.
>
> I once saw myself as somewhat separate from the rest, now I don't.
>
> I once was hypnotized, now I'm not.
>
> I appear to be profoundly contradicting myself, but I'm not.
>
> I have been on both sides of the line.

My perspective has shifted profoundly, for certain. But what is being viewed has not shifted. Nor has what is viewing it. I am fundamentally exactly the same as I have always been and *this* is fundamentally exactly the same as it has always been. Everything that has changed has only been cosmetic. Of no real consequence in the big picture.

So, what does it all mean in the end? What does it mean to go from poverty to great wealth? From misery to happiness? From loneliness to love? From inner conflict to peace? From hypnosis to awakening? Nothing at all.

Every move is a lateral move within the chessboard of the mind, but the only position we can ever occupy is Square One. Here and Now, this is the only spot where we ever get to stand. And what you have, what you feel or what you perceive changes absolutely nothing about the Here and Now.

It's all the same. Just a game. And every move serves to achieve only one objective. To bring us right back to the start. Moment after moment after moment…

Chapter 7

THERE ARE NO MASTERS

In the land of the blind, as the author H.G. Wells told us over a century ago, the one-eyed man is king.[14] In his story, though, the one-eyed man was far from a king in a land of skillfully adapted blind citizens. The role of the spiritual guru has become one of the most dishonest professions there is. Many of the one-eyed men and women who would presume to lead the so-called 'blind' and dare to assume authority over their lives, are charlatans at best and maniacs at worst.

There was a time when society was structured feudally and these sorts of roles of authority existed in all aspects of life. There were the feudal lords who exercised power and authority over the serfs. There were caste systems in place that organized humanity into a hierarchy from 'most human' to 'least human', with the former being treated like kings and the latter worse than animals.

It is precisely from this era that the roles of *guru* and *sishya*—master and student—emerged. At a time when one human being assuming absolute control and authority over another was the norm, this sort of relationship made sense. It was congruous with the times. Yet, the fact that this dynamic has survived, and continues to thrive, well into the 21st century is an aberration of epic proportions.

That would be like finding out that serfdom still exists. Or that the caste system still thrives. In fact, in certain rural parts in the interior of India there are often reports of honor killings

14. 'The Country of the Blind', a short story by H. G. Wells first published in the April 1904 issue of *The Strand Magazine*.

based on a person's caste. And when we read this sort of thing in the news it repulses us on a very deep level. Similarly, when we hear about the treatment of women as conquests of war and sex slaves by militant groups, it causes a visceral rage reflex within us because of the sheer indignation that such ignorance still has a place in our world.

And yet, we see millions of highly educated, well-to-do people, raised within a scientific society, in the first world, succumbing to such archaic and primitive behavior as perpetuating this horribly outdated guru-disciple tradition by handing over all power, dignity, authority (and money) to some douchebag in a robe or loincloth or suit or other garb.

Today, contemporary spirituality, as an industry, generates over 10 billion dollars in books in the US alone and is estimated to be worth over 50 billion dollars worldwide. The wellness industry itself, of which spirituality is a niche driver, is worth over 3.4 trillion dollars today.

What this means is that there are some seriously rich one-eyed motherfuckers walking this earth today. Enlightenment never looked so lucrative. Meanwhile, old Buddha died a poor sod.

Yet, unlike other industries, such as the tech industry, that have something to show for all the investment, products and money being made, the spiritual and self-help industries have achieved very little. We could compare them to pyramid schemes, that promise greater returns for increasing investments but in the end collapse and leave us all empty, in debt and with nothing to show for our 'investment'.

Here's the baseline reality: this is a *farming* operation. And like good fat cattle, consumers of this industry are led out to pasture each day to feed on the delicious, nutritionally empty, rhetoric of the masters and experts. Then they are led back to the barn to be milked.

The feed comes in so many flavors, shapes and colors that

some people spend a lifetime going out to pasture and gorging on spiritual gummy bears: water and sugar, to stunt your growth, encourage an infantile dependency in mind, body and heart.

I say, 'Fuck those masters!'

What does it mean to master something? It means to own it, to conquer it, to dominate it. You can master a skill, master an art, master a process, but mastering another human being? That is some twisted shit.

There are no masters and students in this equation, only masters and slaves. Anytime you hear someone calling themselves a master (or guru)—run! Run far the fuck away. Nothing good will ever come of it.

There is only one master here and that is life itself. Life owns us, it dominates us, it grants us the gift of yet another day and it gives us the pink slip without warning when the time comes. Many people are slaves to it but some of us are its students. We accept its revelations with gratitude and take its lumps without so much as a whimper. Absolutely everything that happens is a lesson in progress. And we are *present,* not because being present is cool, or spiritual or like totally woke or some such nonsense. But because this is class and we are 'paying attention' to the lesson. Can't pay attention if you're daydreaming.

7.8 billion students, a few present, most absent. But no masters among them. Not a single one. And as for those 'one-eyed' smart asses pretending to be the teacher's pet and trying to exercise authority over the others?

Wait for the recess and we'll take care of business in the schoolyard.

CHAPTER 8

BE AS YOU ARE

Q: All these spiritual teachings have me tied up in knots man… It's hard to tell what's up or down these days…is this all an illusion?… is there any choice here?… I'm struggling to move forward coz these questions make me second-guess myself.

Going through a custody battle right now… I want to see my kids so bad… but then it's like, is there really a choice in all this?… do I give up and just see what happens?… do I fight for them?… does it matter?… am I just clinging to attachments?… is this just my ego?

I feel paralyzed by the confusion….

A: All the wisdom teachings in the world pale in comparison to the wisdom of our own intuition. It sounds to me like we've lost touch with that, because we've got into the habit of replacing our inner compass with ready-made mass-produced (brought out by others) maps.

It so happened the other day that a friend and I were driving in his car in an area with which we were unfamiliar, when his phone, which he'd been using as a GPS, suddenly died. And he began freaking out because he had no idea where he was and how we were going to get back home.I asked him how he had functioned in the days when things like GPS were not easily available.

I watched as some ancient faculty in his brain gradually awoke and he began to use his native intelligence: identifying things like landmarks, spatial orientation with respect to the mountains, the arc of the sun and his memory of familiar-looking paths, to bring us back to where we were staying. And at the end he was quite astonished at how this latent ability within him had become dormant while he relied on external guidance systems to direct him.

All the questions we are asking here—you can think of them in those silent times when you are alone—are ultimately nonsensical: Is this an illusion? Is there any choice? Does it matter? Are you clinging? Is this ego? If it is ego then what do I mean by ego? There is absolutely no practical value whatsoever to asking these questions.

There is an introspective value to such questions, however. Yet, at the same time, the introspective value lies *not* in answering the questions but in how we push ourselves to probe more deeply into ourself. The question is not even the point. The motivation is the point—it's the motivation that it stirs within us. The questions aren't so much the point, but the importance is how they get us to question ourselves in so many different ways: to take an open perspective, to question our very lives. The question itself is almost rhetorical.

Is this an illusion? The way to deal with this question is to riposte with another question such as: *What does it feel like to you?* That is where the question is going—not looking for some feeble generic answer for you to chew its cud like some willing sheep. Forget about what it 'is' according to some ancient text or some neuroscientific discovery. Does it *feel* like an illusion? Because remember—both your body and much of your brain are responding to what reality feels like, not what reality *is*.

If I tell you that this chair is made up of trillions of atoms which are in turn mostly made up of space, how is this information useful to you if all you need is something solid to sit on? And if you were to take this information and become paralyzed about whether to sit or not to sit, based on what the true nature of that chair is, how absurd would that be?

No matter what your rational brain thinks of the chair, your ass—your rear end—is going to think it's a solid reliable surface to rest on every single time.

So, forget all the bullshit philosophizing about what the nature of reality is and so on and get down to the bare bones of what it is you *feel* most strongly in your gut. That, and not some dead sage's teachings, is what is going to help you navigate this challenging personal situation that you and your ex-wife are in with regards to the custody of your kids. This is about how life 'works' for you.

To me the only statement that contained any shred of certainty and confidence in your question was: 'I want to see my kids so bad.' Out of the mess of confusion that one statement rings out like a bell. Why second guess the only thing you are clear about?

Is this just clinging to attachments? Is this just your ego? So what if it is?

If your kids grow up knowing that their father fought to stay in their lives do you think they're really going to care if you 'had attachments'? Or if 'your ego made you do it'?

Don't discount the wisdom of your body. It's much smarter than we give it credit for. While our rational brains are great at working in abstract spaces of theory and possibility, nothing understands the reality of the situation better than the body. It already knows what needs to be done.

That's why we use phrases like 'gut feeling' and 'feeling it in the bones', 'I felt it in my waters'. Its raw, native intelligence is much more grounded than all the advanced mental strategies and thought processes we indulge in that we give far too much credit to.

I once watched a mother duck fight off a fucking cobra because of that one sentiment of: *I want to see my kids so bad*. This is an intelligence hardwired into you at the genetic level. If you want to follow scripture, read *that* code.

Now, I'm not saying that the wisdom of all these spiritual

teachings and so on are hogwash. But we must arrive there organically, not have them enforced upon our life.

Something like the 'giving up of attachments' must happen as organically as an apple falls by itself from the tree when it has ripened in its own juices and grown too heavy for the tree to bear. Until that point, its 'attachment' to the tree is necessary in order for nature to take its course. Plucking it preemptively kills that process.

Where I live in northern Japan, I am surrounded by rice paddies. It's spring now and all the farmers are out wading into the fields planting little shoots and submerging them under water. In other words, they are out 'creating attachments'.

And as spring turns into summer, the water levels in the fields will go down and the rice plants will emerge taller, stronger and lusher. Their attachments to the soil will be stronger than ever.

But by the time autumn comes around, those same rice plants will have turned yellow. And the same farmers will go out into the fields with their scythes and 'sever all those attachments' in order to harvest the grain.

And in winter, these fields will be bare and covered in pristine snow, devoid of all attachments altogether. They will also be devoid of much life and vibrancy.

The farmers understand this.

Only a foolish farmer would go out into the fields in the summer with his scythe and start hacking at his rice plants before they have even had a chance to develop any grain. Only a misguided farmer would go tramping in the snow in the winter trying to plant tender shoots of rice into frozen ground.

There is a time for everything.

The dropping away of attachments is something that happens organically at a certain stage in a person's maturity. To try and make it happen preemptively is to misunderstand the wisdom of the process entirely.

So, if some sage is talking about the illusory nature of life and his lack of attachments, then that's where he is at *in his own process*. It may be of some relevance if you find yourself at a similar place in your own life. Otherwise, it is nothing more than academic.

It could be a blistering hot day in the northern hemisphere where you are. Meanwhile, some wise dude living in New Zealand, where it's winter, might be dressed in a winter jacket. Does that mean you need to become confused about what attire to wear? Whether you also should be bundling up? That's absurd.

A cold winter in New Zealand is *not* where you are at. That's where he is at. You are in the midst of a blistering summer. Shorts and a t-shirt are what you need. And if there is any question about it, check with your body and it will illustrate the solution quite accurately for you.

Be as you are.

And operate from there. Through the process of living, those other profound questions will start becoming apparent and revealing themselves to you in their own time. And even if they don't, what does it matter? There is no finish line. No award to receive for your efforts. No one is going to pat you on the back for having answered them.

The only reward you ever get to enjoy is this single space and moment of where you are right now. Sit your ass on that seat. Own it. And then command your path forward from there.

When it comes to this big show we call life:

It's better to have your own seat, even if it's up in the nose bleeds, than to spend your time in the front row sitting on someone else's lap.

CHAPTER 9

ALWAYS PRESENT

Q: I've spent so much of my life attempting to stay present by keeping my mind at bay. At the end of it, I feel totally exhausted. But what's worse is that I don't seem to know my own mind anymore. What makes me happy, what motivates me, what kinds of relationships matter, how do I express my creativity? I used to have a sense of this in my younger days. Now, I feel like this whole spiritual path for me has just sanitized all of that out. The good and the bad.

How can I remain present and still allow the mind to function? To me they always seem mutually exclusive? Can you help me resolve this conflict? Maybe I'm missing something…?

A: It's not so much something you are missing as it is something you are overlooking. It is actually there, but you are directing your attention—focusing on—something else.

It happens to me all the time when I'm in a hurry to get out of the house and the set of car keys I'm looking for are already in my hand. When we attempt to 'stay present' we are working on the assumption, whether consciously or unconsciously, that we are not present to start with.

We've taken on these assumptions from all kinds of spiritual books and new age philosophies which are invested in defending a status quo that they have established with a narrow and restricted view of things.

As a result, people who attempt to order and control their lives by the focus that these philosophies promote are likely to live narrow and restricted inner lives.

As with most of life's challenges, when something feels amiss it helps to get down to the very basics and question those deeply-rooted assumptions which—as assumptions usually do—lurk below the radar of our day-to-day awareness. In this case, you have made the assumption that *I am not present*.

So, my question to you is: *How do you know this? What is the definition of 'being present'?*

Now, you may respond with something like: *I find myself often distracted from my circumstances. I'm lost in thought or fantasy or projecting scenarios of doom and gloom.* Or: *I'm getting carried away with my emotions rather than simply noticing what is around me. I find myself living in a make-believe world in my mind in which things are going wrong while the reality of my actual life is quite simple.*

This is pretty much why most people want to be present, isn't it? To be spared the anxieties of the mind?

So, here we arrive at another basic assumption: being in the real world implies presence whereas being in the thought-based world of the mind is absence.

But let's think about this for a second. Let's say you leave your home and go to the office. I can truthfully say that she is present at work and absent at home. But can I truthfully say she is only absent or only present?

Those are blanket statements that preclude a context where none is provided. The truth is best described by saying that in order to be present at home you have no choice but to be absent at work. And in order to be present at work you have no choice but to be absent from home. With particular reference to the Covid-19 crisis, you may be in a work from home scenario, in which case you may be present in both. Yet, you will undoubtedly have to attend to either housework or office work by taking turns being present in one or the other.

The point is someone defining being present as being mindful of one's immediate physical circumstances is like saying one is only considered present if one is at home. That makes no sense.

The immediate physical circumstance is only one of the many realities we have the ability to inhabit. If I'm daydreaming instead of doing the dishes, you may admonish me for not being present in my physical circumstances but I would say that that's because I'm busy being present with my thoughts. Or if I'm raging at some insult or circumstance, I would say I'm being present with my anger.

In fact, presence is the standard default setting. You, I, and everyone we meet is always present in their lives. Which layer of reality we are present in, that's the thing that is subject to change.

Whether you are lost in an effervescent emotion such as anger, or in some fantasy about a future you hope will come true, or simply being mindful of the soapy suds covering your hands as you lather the dishes: you are no more and no less present in any of these scenarios. What changes is what you are present with. Are you present with your thoughts, present with your emotions or present with your circumstances?

The way I see it presence is simple—it's merely the awareness of what is happening. That 'happening' may be something physical, something emotional or something mental, or some kind of combination.

Now, there is some value to developing the skill of being mindful of one's physical circumstances. Contrary to what anyone might say, this is not because the physical reality is superior or somehow more real than any other. It's simply that it is the most stable by far.

If you think of physical reality as the ground we stand on, then our emotional reality is like the ocean and our mental reality is like the sky. Of these three planes, land is by far the most stable. The ocean is more challenging to traverse due to its unpredictable swells and tides. But, the sky is the most challenging of all because it seems limitless.

Being able to return to land whenever necessary is just a prudent strategy. It allows for a less harrowing day-to-day experience of life. You aren't navigating endless waters wondering when you will see land or flying over a vast expanse of sky wondering if you'll run out of fuel and have to attempt a crash landing.

But, none of this implies that staying on land is somehow a superior way to be than sailing on the ocean or flying in the sky. That kind of thinking just grounds you, but not in a good way. It's like a pilot refusing to get in an airplane or a sailor refusing to get on a ship because he thinks that land is the only reality. That's rubbish.

You are always present. Present with your thoughts, present with your emotions, present with your circumstances. What you are struggling to achieve here is balance, not presence.

Spending too much time in your head alienates you from your immediate environment. Spending too much time absorbed in your immediate circumstances alienates you from your imagination. So, it seems to me, having spent a great part of your life in the first scenario, the pendulum has now swung to the second scenario.

Let go of these dictates telling you how to be and realize that being is what is happening anyways. There is no real 'how' to it and it can't stop happening. Relaxing that pressure will allow the pendulum to gradually come to rest at its own centre point, whatever that may be. That is how you will learn to find your own balance. By finding that centre point—finding it for yourself and then using it as your benchmark—not by following what some book or teacher says it must be.

Chapter 10

AWAKENING VS. THE ART OF LIVING

Q. What is the correlation between awakening and living a good life? So, many so-called 'enlightened masters' turn out to be absolutely terrible people. It seems like a massive contradiction to me. Doesn't awakening make someone a better person?

A: This is a question that strikes at the heart of a fundamental misconception: that awakening to reality and one's true nature also provides solutions to human dilemmas and reveals the secrets of wellbeing and the art of living.

So, I'm going to try and clarify this misunderstanding. Because in my experience, awakening, wellbeing and the art of living are not the same things, even if they may be somewhat loosely connected.

To begin, let's discuss what we mean by these terms.

Awakening

I would describe awakening as:

> *A moment-in-time event in which something fundamental and hidden about the nature of reality and self is suddenly and spontaneously revealed.*

Thus, awakening is an experience. The experience can range from no more than a few seconds to several months (as was in my case) or longer. Regardless of how long such awakening experiences last, they do end. Yet, they have a lasting effect on the person's life and overall outlook.

These are some of the experiences that happened during my awakening. They concur with the experience of others, who have spoken about their own experiences, too:

> There is a clear and sudden interruption to the usual functioning of the brain.
>
> The personality, while still functioning, becomes significantly disabled.
>
> Thoughts cease abruptly and silence rushes to the forefront and remains there with no effort.
>
> Sensory perceptions become enhanced: colors become more vivid, sounds more acute.
>
> Everything brims with a sense of immediacy.
>
> The commonly experienced sense of self gives way to a much wider and less definable sense of being that seems to encompass not only oneself but all that one perceives.
>
> Everything feels alive, conscious and familiar, including inanimate objects.
>
> There is an overwhelming sense of familiarity, friendship and love for everything.
>
> There is humor in everything, even the dull and mundane.
>
> Fear, worry, anxiety seem baseless and strangely alien.

> I'm effortlessly, continuously and totally physically present and that doesn't change for the entire duration of the awakening.
>
> I perceive the speech and actions of other people as caricatures: like second-rate acting in a substandard play. I often want to shake other people and tell them to snap out of their scripts.
>
> I feel awkward talking to people because even my own words and mannerisms feel strange, alien and put on.
>
> Thoughts take effort to think, words take effort to speak and actions take effort to perform.
>
> My automatic natural resting state, when there are no external demands requiring my attention, is one of relaxed, inactive, silent and empty witnessing. (Like a house cat gazing out the window all day.)
>
> I do not feel a sense of being separate from life, nor do I feel as if I have any real will or volition of my own.
>
> Everything seems to happen spontaneously, while all I can do is to watch as it happens.

The reason I say that awakening is a moment-in-time event with a shelf-life stamped on it, is because of what causes such an experience to happen in the first place.

It seems that an awakening results when the rational/analytical hemisphere of the brain, in which the ego resides, becomes partially disabled. This often happens due to some intense trauma that causes a breakdown. Two examples come to mind here; firstly, that of Eckart Tolle, who claims to have experienced his awakening after a period of severe depression. The second refers to Dr Jill Bolte Taylor who experienced her awakening after a cerebrovascular accident (stroke).

Yet, eventually the brain may regain its functions. When it does, the ego kicks back into gear along with the rational/analytical processes which employ a steady stream of thought to project simulated models of reality. This is useful to anticipate dangers, mitigate risks and promote safety and survival.

Thus, the awakening experience ends and the system regains standard operations. However, the individual person remains fundamentally changed in some ways as a result of the experience. What we have witnessed, heard, felt and experienced can never be unseen or undone.

The Art of Living

The Art of Living should really be 'The Art of Living Well', because that's essentially what we are alluding to when we call something an art. We are pointing to a certain degree of mastery. I would approach a definition as follows:

> *A well-lived life is one which is lived fully. It's a life in which joys and sorrows, trials and triumphs, peaks and troughs are all experienced and embraced in such a manner that we are left feeling enriched by them rather than impoverished—with few or no regrets. The predominant experience, in such a life, is one of flow and a feeling of genuine connection with* what *is.*
>
> *Ordinary moments are no less precious than extraordinary ones. Ordinary people, events and places are no less significant than so-called 'extraordinary' ones. There is a great simplicity to living such a life. And a light-heartedness which infuses itself into life's circumstances and lightens their burden.*

Yet, there is a seriousness in approach. We face life squarely, refusing to look away from it. We take full responsibility not only for ourselves but also for *What Is* as it appears. This includes the people, places, things and events that inhabit our life. We realize that the buck ultimately stops at our own perception of things. Thus, shame and blame have no base from which to operate.

We honor our relationships, our promises, ourselves. Character, integrity and a clear personal ethical standard are hallmarks. There is no room for hypocrisy. Truth and sincerity of expression are non-negotiables. This is the uncompromising bar we set.

This is a life that seeks willfully to harm no one. Nor do we seek willfully to help others based on some idealistic notion of being altruistic. We simply act spontaneously and with clear determination.

Integrity of character can only follow if there has been an integration of all the fragments of the self. Therefore, those who have come full circle into themselves, have reconciled the darkness within, have bridged the chasm between their apparent and ideal selves, can be said to be 'whole' beings. Wholeness is the prerequisite foundation of a good life. Until then, one is incomplete. And that incompletion always seeks to resolve itself by projecting a 'not good enough' outwards.

Balance is a fundamental feature of a good life. Yet, when such a balance is artificially imposed or externally dictated, according to a set of rules, it does not result in harmony. It creates a tentative equilibrium which is shaky at best and can be thrown off balance by any number of factors, both internal and external. Balance only results when a person is deeply grounded, with a sense of the gravity of his or her whole being. Thus, balance cannot manifest without a foundation of wholeness as its basis.

Some of the hallmarks of artful living include: acceptance,

flow, simplicity, humor, courage, accountability, integrity, sincerity, wholeness and balance.

Chapter 11

THE STORY OF THE GAMER

Having outlined my perspectives on awakening and the art of living , it's time to talk about how they are related.

So, let's consider the story of the gamer:

Imagine a group of Virtual Reality (VR) gamers who live in the 22nd century. Our gamers spend their entire lives playing just one game. They've played it all day, every day: they can't remember a day when they did not play it. They know nothing about another reality, beyond their VR: a place where their bodies 'really' exist. They identify completely with their virtual avatars (ie, their first-person protagonist in the story of the game world they are inhabiting).

Let's imagine now that there's a gamer whose VR system briefly sparks out. And when this malfunction happens, one side of his VR headset fails to display his virtual world; instead it reveals the world he 'really' inhabits. Our gamer suddenly finds himself living in an 'augmented reality', with one half of his perception in the virtual world as his avatar and the other half of his vision in the real world as himself.

Glimpsing a more fundamental reality and experiencing a self not limited by his avatar is a revelation. For a while he is transfixed by this alternate perception and he could not care less about the game and what is happening within it. Soon, though, the VR system regains its full function, the partial view of the fundamental reality becomes obscured and the virtual reality takes over again. Yet, he will always retain his feel for the base reality that he glimpsed so fleetingly.

Here are some questions that our gamer (or we ourselves) may pose in the light of this example:

How does the gamer go back to playing the game?

Will this experience improve his gameplay, negatively impact it or make no difference?

What motivations will drive him forward in the gameplay?

The Aftermath

The questions that follow the analogy above are essentially the same ones we need to consider when talking about awakening and the art of living. Because while awakening has to do with perceiving a fundamental reality beyond this 'game of life', the art of living is all about playing the "game of life" well.

And in that sense there is no way to determine how awakening will impact one's ability to live. Some of the impacts could be wholly negative.

For example, after his revelation, the gamer may feel deeply bored, frustrated and cynical about having to be stuck playing a game which now feels pointless and entirely artificial. He may instead, decide to go berserk and start killing off various characters in the game and break every rule of gameplay there is. (There are those who turn highly destructive and antisocial following an awakening).

Or perhaps, after his revelation, the gamer may go in search of some path within the game that can cause a similar glitch to occur that will disable the VR system. He may find other characters that claim to have experienced something similar or even those who promise to be able to show him how to achieve it. (Many people immerse themselves into spirituality or follow gurus in order to try and regain the perspective revealed to them during awakening).

Or perhaps, he will remain disoriented for sometime and fail to really get a handle on how to play out the rest of his existence in the game world. He may drift in a sort of aimless limbo moving from one distraction to another in order to dull his confusion. (Listlessness and a sense of limbo are common experiences after awakening).

Or perhaps, he may realize it's just a game so he needn't feel any sense of empathy or accountability for anyone. No longer hinged to a conscience, he may find himself driven by a desire for power and decide to bend and break whatever rules he needs to in order to dominate the game by manipulating other players and bending their will to his. (Some will set themselves up as gurus or spiritual leaders and seek to consolidate power at the expense of others).

All of the examples above are ways in which one could potentially go off in a wholly negative direction following an awakening. In fact, there have been plenty of people who have had exactly these outcomes happen.

So, clearly awakening by no mean implies that one will get any better at living life. And it certainly provides no solutions to many of the dilemmas of being human nor reveals the secrets to living a good life.

The Correlation

But there is a link between awakening and the art of living. And that is they share the same essence.

The problem that people who have experienced an awakening face is that they become obsessed with replicating the experience. But not only is this impractical it's also undesirable. The awakening is designed to provide a glimpse of the essence of reality. In order to do that certain brain functions (especially the ego function) need to be temporarily disabled because they tend to operate at odds with the holistic view. Yet, once they turn back on, we may mistakenly interpret that as an error that needs to be rectified. And so we may embark on a spiritual path whose goal is to turn off all those interfering functions in order to return to that awakened state.

This is backward thinking.

When I was in the 10th grade, my uncle, who was a heart surgeon, took me with him to his hospital in Chicago to shadow him for eighteen hours of back to back surgery. His goal was to give me a glimpse of what a day in the life of a cardiac surgeon was like (since I had been contemplating a career in medicine at the time). For those eighteen hours, I wore scrubs, a doctor's coat and was addressed by all the staff and technicians as an equal—as if I were a resident doctor. I witnessed six surgeries standing right by the patients each time. I even stood there while my uncle gave hope to families with loved ones in surgery or expressed regret as they broke down in his arms. For those eighteen hours, I glimpsed what the life of a surgeon was like.

Now, imagine if I had been inspired to pursue a career as a surgeon after that (which I incidentally didn't). What would I have to do in order to 'get back' into that surgery room? The path I'd have to follow would need to be an entirely different one than what took me into that room the first time. But if I misunderstood that, then I might struggle for a very long time. I might keep donning a fake gown and mask and try breaking into surgery and pretending to be a surgeon. And if I somehow managed to pull that off without getting caught, I'd most likely end up doing a lot of harm to any patients I treated.

What is 'required' to get back into that surgery room, then, is a path of growth, learning, mastery and maturity. And if I ever found myself back in the surgery room after that it would be because I belonged there and not because I just accidentally arrived there.

Similarly, awakening provides a glimpse of an essence that is possible to experience in the everyday human reality we live in. Yet, the context is a wholly different one. When essence is confused with context, a whole Pandora's box of confusions emerge.

The Inspiration

Awakening provides a certain perspective on life which, when considered in the right context, can enhance our attitude towards life itself.

So, for example, our gamer, having experienced his revelation, after a certain period of disorientation, immerses himself into playing the game once again. He does this not to learn how to win or to dominate or to achieve any of the goals that once drove him, but rather for a renewed love of the game itself. Realizing it is just a game allows him to approach it with a certain lightness of heart. Yet, he takes the gameplay 100% seriously. He is free of the belief that anything in the game is representative of the truth and yet also understands that truth must be fundamental to everything he does.

Awakening can be used as a tool to try and dominate life or it can be used as a means of deepening our relationship with it.

There are hundreds of people who have mastered the art of living yet have never had an awakening. Still, they naturally operate in a manner that is truly harmonious with life.

Then there are people who have had tremendous revelations and profound glimpses into reality and self, yet are people whom you couldn't trust as far as you could throw them (an endless laundry list of gurus comes to mind).

Mastery of the art of living appears to happen as a consequence of experience, wisdom, age, maturity, integrity, balance and wholeness.

Awakening doesn't cause any of those things.

At worst, awakening will motivate us in a direction that seeks to negate all life in an effort to regain that single moment in time and hold it frozen in our vision forever.

At best, awakening may motivate us in a direction that seeks to learn how to live well. To manifest in human terms what we have witnessed beyond it.

Chapter 12

SOMETHING MISSING

On a withered branch
A crow has alighted;
Nightfall in autumn.

—Basho[15]

J: I'm so tired of this non-duality bullshit, man… I've read all the books, spent hundreds of hours meditating, hundreds of hours watching videos, hundreds of hours doing self-inquiry… I think I have burnt myself out, man. I really do.

I feel like the 'withered branch' in that Zen poem.

I can't do it anymore. I know it's coming to an end… and that scares me.

I know I can't do what I've been doing… but I know seeking won't end at the same time.

I'm fucked.

Sorry for bothering you with this shit, brother. No need to reply. I guess it was more a statement to myself than a question directed at you.

AA: What are you seeking, J?

J: I really don't know. I guess an end to seeking.

AA: End to seeking what?

J: To the idea that I can somehow figure it all out. To know what

15. http://oaks.nvg.org/basho.html

'I' am and what the world is.

AA: You know what the 'I' is and what the world is.

J: Do I?

AA: Look around you. That's the world.
What's looking? That's you.
A two-year-old knows this…

J: Yes indeed. But then why do I feel like that's not enough?

AA: That's the more important question.
So, what are you *really* seeking, J?

J: Why the fuck am I driving myself insane looking for something that doesn't exist?

AA: What's this something that may or may not exist?

J: …

AA: Did you ever feel scared as a kid?

J: Not often but yes.

AA: I remember the feeling of standing above the diving board at our pool and being terrified to jump. And all I wanted was to know that it was going to turn out ok.

J: So I'm that kid…

AA: Everybody man. Everybody is that kid. Science, religion, technology, spirituality, everything in society is driven by this one basic desire.

To know just a bit more, so I can comfort that kid.

We are all fucking scared.

Because no one knows how the fuck any of us got here and where all this is headed.

It's like waking up from a coma and finding yourself in some twilight zone.

That's what life is... a twilight zone with no beginning or end.

Just some bizarre middle we all have learned to pretend isn't so bizarre.

J: I already knew that.

AA: Great.

J: So then what the fuck is the point?

AA: Point of what?

J: All of it.

AA: Who said there is one? It's like me taking my kids to the park and putting them in the sandbox.

And if one of them were to ask me, 'What the fuck is the point of this?'

What can I say?

I dunno... What's the point for you?

J: I get what you're saying.

But somehow that's not satisfying.

I still feel like I'm missing something.

I don't know what.

AA: You've left home and can't remember if you left the stove on…

Something is missing always.

Certainty.

That's the only thing anyone craves.

I'd rather believe I'm going to a hell than not know…

J: Yes… *this* is it… but what the fuck *is* this??

AA: Who says it's a what?

Call it whatever you want. A rose by any other name and all that…

J: 'Who says it's a what?'

That's interesting. I can't answer that. Lol.

AA: Are you okay with not being able to answer that?

J: So basically this is it and I will never be able to answer that question…

I would have to say no. I'm still not okay with that for some reason.

AA: Do you want to be okay with it?

J: Yes.

AA: So it's not the so-called 'reason' that matters to you. It's the feeling of being okay that's driving it.

If it was knowing what all of this was really about, then you'd say, 'No! I don't want to be fucking okay with anything. I want to fucking know, regardless of how I'm going to feel about knowing.'

Fair assessment?

J: Yes.

AA: So this search has never been about knowing. Knowing was just the tool you figured would help you get to that feeling of being OK.

The tool didn't work.
Fuck it.
Who said you even need a tool?
Maybe there is a direct way to access the okayness.
With me?

J: Yes I'm with you.

AA: How's your financial situation if you don't mind me asking? No need for details. Are you hard up, not bad, doing well?

J: It's alright. I get by.
Why?

AA: Gotcha. Things could be better, but things could be a lot worse. Fair?

J: Yes.

AA: That's basically the definition of 'okay'.
Next, health wise. How you doing?

J: Right, lol.
You really want a breakdown of my personal shit?

AA: Just general buckets. Unless it's too much work…

J: I've been better physically… I drink and smoke too much.

AA: Do you feel impaired or impeded in any way in your day to day?

J: Trying to get back in shape so yes…
But generally I'm 'okay'.

AA: Sure. See where I'm going with this?

J: Yes and no.
You're saying why bother…

AA: Why bother with what?

J: 'Okay' somehow isn't enough, man…

AA: 'More than okay', then?

J: I don't care about money, women, status etc.

AA: What is enough for you? How would you define enough?

J: I just want to know what the fuck *this* is.

AA: Why do you want to know?

J: Lol.
You're funny!
How to feel okay…
Fuck!

AA: See the circle of logic?

J: I see it. But it's never-ending.

AA: Of course. Where is the end of a circle? Lol.

Fuckin' hamsters on the wheel don't get that concept do they?

J: So just stop.

Then my mind says that's not enough...

And back on the wheel again...

AA: Of course. Because when you stop the whole thing ends.

'This is the end
Beautiful friend.
This is the end
My only friend, the end.
Of all elaborate plans, the end.
Of everything that stands,
The end.'[16]

J: The Doors?

AA: Yup. That's why the search is an addiction, mate. Because even when you see that it's going nowhere, you keep hopping back on that wheel...

J: Definitely.

So how did you hop off?

AA: Step 1[17]. Admit the search is not the solution. It *is* the problem.

J: I know this.

16. *The End* by the Doors (Jim Morrison, Ray Manzarek, Robby Krieger, John Densmore) from the album *The Doors*. Released January 4, 1967. Hollywood, California, August 1966. Elektra.

17. Step I: *"We admitted we were powerless (over alcohol)—that our lives had become unmanageable."* *The Big Book of Alcoholics Anonymous* by Bill Wilson et al.

AA: Step 2. Admit the problem is the same as any addict has. Nothing more special about you just cuz you all spiritual and shit…

You're a junkie like every alcoholic and crackhead out there.

J: That's obvious too.

AA: Step 3. Admit that there is no answer to the what's missing.

J: …

AA: Step 4. *Sit* with what's missing until you *are* what's missing.

All there is to it.

Very simple.

Just not easy.

J: Why do I still feel like there's an answer to what's missing?

AA: Because you haven't yet fully taken Step 1.

There can be no getting off the wheel until you fully get that it's going nowhere.

Until then, all you are really doing is sticking one leg out to slow it down because it's getting too quick for you…

So the frustration you are feeling with the search is good but it's not quite there yet.

Not frustrated enough.

J: Fuck!

AA: Fuck is good.

J: Tell me something. Why do you share your perspective? What do you hope to gain or accomplish by sharing your views? If anything…

AA: Why do you breathe?

J: Lol. That simple, eh?

AA: Always and only.

Chapter 13
MORALLY BANKRUPT TEACHERS

Q: Why are so many spiritual teachers morally bankrupt individuals?

A: This is a fascinating question and deserves a multifaceted answer precisely because there are a number of factors that contribute to this moral bankruptcy.

Firstly, seekers on the spiritual path may arrive at a point when they realize that life is inherently meaningless. And since this is the case, what we call morality is just a bunch of rules that were made up to facilitate a more pleasant experience of living with our fellow humans. But morality is by no means something that is set in stone. For someone who has suffered from feelings of shame and low self-esteem this can come as a tremendously liberating realization. (Many seekers do emerge from this sort of broken background.)

As a result of such a realization, a seeker who then sets up as a teacher may assume an 'anything goes' sort of attitude towards morality and sexuality. Having seen through the facade of ordinary morality and ethics they see no reason to adhere to it. Yet, the strange irony is that those relaxed rules only really apply to them. The people around them and especially followers are often expected to operate within a strict code of conduct, especially in relation to the teacher.

For example, verbally abusing, publicly humiliating, sexually exploiting or taking financial advantage of a student is acceptable if it suits the needs of the teacher since right and wrong are labelled as projections of a mind that is still trapped in a conditioned paradigm of morality. Yet, how many of those very teachers would, likewise, be okay with being verbally abused, publicly humiliated, sexually exploited or taken financial advantage of? Not many!

Such stances are tools that teachers employ, whether intentionally or delusionally, in order to maintain a sense of superiority and control over their students while maintaining a flawless image of transcendence in their own minds.

Secondly, the spiritual path and tradition itself tend to equate morality with mortality. All human endeavor is ultimately linked to our preoccupation with death. If you could distill our human efforts down to their root motivations, survival and reproduction (survival of the blood line) is what it all boils down to. Morality then is a social strategy to maximize our survival and thereby deny (albeit temporarily) our own looming demise. How many people actually live like they are never going to die? A lot more than would admit. Our own death is more a hypothetical scenario than a real possibility to us. It is an intellectual event at best.

Spirituality in all its forms is about realizing our immortality. No matter how you approach it: whether in the Christian sense of a soul that lives forever in the afterlife, or the Buddhist/ Hindu sense of a sequence of algorithmic *vasanas* recreating lifetimes in order to resolve themselves, there is a sense of continuity beyond the human form of this lifetime.

As a result, we expect our enlightened men and women to have transcended the mortal plane, and realized the immortal within themselves, while living in human bodies on earth. Because we equate morality with mortality, we also expect them to be beyond our ordinary notions of good and evil. We perceive them as being pure in all that they think, say and do. Rather than evaluating them based on their actions, like we would with other people, we place such individuals beyond evaluation altogether.

Thus, anyone claiming enlightenment realizes that an amoral outlook and demeanor comes with the job description. And any immoral behavior can easily be rationalized away as being simply amoral: a spontaneous emergence of life through the vessel of the individual.

As the Buddhist teacher Sogyal Rinpoche would allegedly remark to his young female assistants whom he would request to clean his arse after taking a shit: 'Even my turds are enlightened.'[18]

Third, the above is a segue into the next reason, which is that many people who pursue the role of spiritual teacher exhibit signs of dysfunctional issues such as borderline personality or narcissistic personality disorders and complexes (such as messiah or god complex, which are often part of other disorders).

These individuals often exhibit higher than average levels of intelligence and communication skills. As a result, they can be highly charismatic. The unique concoction of these disorders and high intelligence creates a paradoxical personality that many find irresistible. This charisma then becomes a double-edged sword because these teachers then take their attraction and appeal as validation for their delusional thinking.

If I believe I can fly like a bird and somehow convince myself of it, it requires daily effort for me to maintain this delusion in my mind. But if I can somehow convince a hundred thousand followers of the same thing, I need no longer exercise that sort of effort. The reality of that belief will be echoed back to me a hundred thousand times over on a daily basis. If it was difficult for me to see my own delusions before, it becomes virtually impossible now.

All humans have the capacity for self-deception but those who are truly accomplished in that art no longer have any bearings on how deep they have really gone. Therefore, to expect

18.https://nypost.com/2018/09/23/buddhist-teacher-forced-devotees-into-sex-wiping-his-butt

any form of ethical behavior from such an individual, unless it coincidentally aligns with some kind of self-serving agenda, is futile.

Truly, the only benchmark we need for evaluating a teacher is, 'How open, honest and consistent are they?'

Is this teacher willing to hold himself to the same standards (or lack thereof) of behavior to which he holds others? Is this teacher willing to analyze himself or be open to the analysis of others to the same extent that he believes others should be open to him? If the teacher has truly transcended fear, is he willing to be open in his own humanness and allow himself to be vulnerable to the criticisms of others rather than building an impervious fortress of defence mechanisms and deflection strategies?

In the end, the issue is not one of morality, immorality or amorality. But rather one of mutual respect. The old adage 'do unto your neighbor as you would have him do unto you' or 'Do as you would be done by' is possibly the wisest and most commonsense advice any of us could follow.

Chapter 14

WHY DO YOU WANT TO WAKE UP?

Q: I can't help but feel extremely frustrated. I have to admit I envy you and others who seem to have awakened. I know you don't claim this as a special achievement or something like that. But to me you don't appear to suffer in the same way I do. Or maybe you used to once upon a time, but not anymore. A part of me knows that this seeking attitude is pointless. But, the craving is still there and I don't know what to do about it. Any pointers?

A: When I was in primary school I attended an all boys English school in Kolkata, India. A vestige of a bygone era when the British still ruled the country, the school operated according to the strictest of rules of decorum and turnout. Corporal punishment was standard fare. Each teacher carried a cane and the principal's office sported an antique oak cabinet that displayed such an assortment of canes and whips as would have put the dungeon of any sadomasochist to shame.

Being the little shithead of a schoolboy I was, I got caned by the teachers on a near daily basis and was sent up to the principal's, for 'Tier 2 Escalation', once a week. In fact, the principal was so familiar with me he would even give me my choice of cane with which to be walloped. But it didn't end there.

Our school was divided into four houses (much like Hogwarts[19]) and each house competed for points throughout the

19. The fictional 'School of Witchcraft and Wizardry' in the Harry

year. Monday mornings were Inspection Day where, in true military style, we'd be lined up by our houses and the principal would inspect our turnout. Were our shirts perfectly starched? Were the creases on our trousers crisp and uniform? Could you see your reflection in our shoes? Those who turned out in exemplary fashion were asked to step forward and earned a precious point for their house. Those who made the cut were passed by. Those who fell short were asked to take a step backwards. In the three years I spent at the school, I was only asked to step forward once.

However, taking a step backwards was almost routine for me. No matter how well dressed I'd be in the morning leaving my home, I couldn't fight my own nature. Somewhere between departing my front door and entering the school gates, I would have transformed from a neatly dressed lad to a raggedy street urchin. The problem was that earning a minus point for your house earned a lot more than that. It earned a sound thrashing from the house prefects (older boys who were assigned to positions of rank and authority within the house).

Now, I know you may be feeling a great deal of sympathy for a young boy who was physically abused on a near daily basis by a horribly antiquated educational system. But please don't. The caning and getting beat up was hardly a deterrent. I barely batted an eyelid. It still never prompted me to turn in my homework on time, or to remember to bring my sports shoes, or to show up on time for drama practice. Besides, all that beating had given me buns o' steel. I could take a flogging full force while saying the alphabet backwards.

Yet, through it all, I felt this deep frustration at the fact that I was just a child. It wasn't so much the physical pain but rather the insult of having no choice but to put up with it. I couldn't wait to be older, like those prefects. They seemed to have it so easy. Every once in a while, I'd see them joking around with a

---

Potter series of books by J.K. Rowling.

teacher almost as equals! I even saw one of them patting the principal's bald head! *In what alternative universe did this sort of freedom and privilege exist?* I would marvel.

And most strikingly of all, there was no corporal punishment for the older boys. When they messed up, at worst they seemed to get a stern talking-to. Perhaps, it was because they were stronger and fiercer, with physiques that rivalled those of the teachers' in power and muscularity. These were some of the ways in which my nine-year-old brain rationalized things.

I never got to become a prefect at that school. We moved constantly in my childhood so by the time I reached high school I was elsewhere. But I did get to grow up as I'd once wished I would. And yet, growing up had nothing to do with how I'd imagined it. I was not getting pushed around, reprimanded and disciplined as much, yet oppression had taken on a different flavor. Being at a top-rated school academically, competition was fierce. There was the burden of social expectations, peer pressure, the obligation to pick a line of study early and work obsessively to master it.

The education system in India at the highest levels is one of the most gruelling and competitive in the world. In order to make it into a half decent university one needs near perfect scores across all subjects (or a shit load of money). Students were battling within decimal percentage points (99.1% to 99.9%, with only anything above 99.5% making it into the top rung of universities). In the 10th grade national exams I had the highest scores in the country in math and English. But by the 11th grade I had stopped giving the kind of fucks I was required to give.

The turning point came when I took my first holiday out of the country to America and saw an entirely different kind of life. That's when I saw the madness of what I was participating in. I promptly followed up on my killer performance in the 10th grade exams, by flunking all five subjects in my 11th grade mid terms.

On that visit to the United States, I'd visited Northwestern University and what I saw there blew my mind. Undergraduate and graduate students from all walks of life: engineers, artists, fashion designers, philosophers, research scientists, anthropologists, literature majors, film students—pursuing whatever their hearts desired (a fairly simplistic view, I know, but that is what it was at the time). While back home, we were all grinding our gears and battling like pit bulls for one of only two options, engineering or medicine, neither of which any of us had any real inkling whether we actually wanted to do.

The old frustration I'd felt as a young boy still burned inside me. I yearned to escape my oppression. I couldn't wait to get older and graduate high school and make decisions that my family would no longer have much of a say in. I was determined never to go to university in India. I knew I needed to get to America somehow before I got swallowed whole.

A few years later, I was attending university in Canada. My lack of extracurricular background during high school meant that I failed to gain entry into the two majors of my choice: journalism and film making. Yet, my robust academic background in the sciences allowed me to major in computer science, my most despised subject of all. I'd always loved math and physics but computers and coding were what I absolutely dreaded.

Here I was, a university student in Canada with all the choices in the world, and I still felt oppressed. I dragged myself to classes where most of what was being taught went sailing over my head. Although I managed to pull out decent grades, primarily because I'd mastered the art of test taking, I can safely say I learned next to nothing in those four years. Still, I pushed through because I knew that it was only four years. Life as an adult in the real world would be completely different. All I needed to do was grow up just a little more, then it would be smooth sailing and open waters ahead. Through those four years my only solace was a great group of friends and my minor in philosophy that helped me to retain my intellectual sanity.

Graduation day came with great pomp and fanfare. I couldn't care less. I was just glad to be set free once and for all. This educational penitentiary that I'd spent most of my life in was behind me. I was paroled. A free man. With no idea what he was going to do. But free nevertheless!I began interviewing for jobs and soon secured an analyst position at a top consulting firm in Toronto's financial district. That turned out to be the job from hell. After a year of working 16-hour days under a tyrannical and paranoid manager, my will had been spent and my self-esteem crushed. I sank into a deep depression.

I began to realize that growing up didn't equate to greater freedom. While greater freedom was a part of it, another part of it was greater burdens of responsibility. Growing up was simply a phenomenon of the stakes going up. It was more like a casino in which you graduate, step by step, to higher stakes tables as your game improves.

In that sense, the oppression I'd felt was *always* going to be a part of the equation. If I wasn't feeling the weight of responsibility, I would most likely be living an unrealistic life of some form of escapism.

But what made that burden oppressive was an attitude of non-acceptance, of resistance. That is why I had never taken responsibility for myself no matter my age or the situation. Instead, I had shirked the responsibility and projected it elsewhere: on a school system that was archaic, or an environment that was ruthlessly competitive or a major that I hated or a job that was soul sucking. While the systemic issues in my environment were no doubt real, the true cause of my suffering was my own unwillingness to take *ownership* of my circumstances.

This is what made me a such a struggler, always fighting against life rather than flowing with it and adapting as necessary. And I recognized that, deep down, I had this irrational desire that life should conform itself to *me*. In fact, it was more than a desire, it was an expectation. A sense of entitlement that plagued me for years.

I'd like to tell you that my awakening in my early twenties changed all that. That with awakening, my sense of being oppressed vanished, my feelings of entitlement or deserving better disappeared. But they didn't. In fact, they became even more acutely difficult for a while. All awakening did was to reveal the nature of my reality to me. Actually, making the hard choices was something that came over time, with maturity and having my ego cut down to size by life's circumstances more often than I care to mention.

The reason I appear not to live in a struggle-based mode today is because I have learned to take responsibility. To take full accountability and ownership of my life's circumstances no matter how pretty or ugly they may appear. While I continue to experience hardship, confusion, disappointment, frustration and so on like any other human being—none of it is oppressive to me anymore. Rather I welcome it because it has been entrusted to me as part and parcel of *What Is*.

I no longer operate within 'should' or 'could' scenarios. Therefore, I no longer project future scenarios in which life could be better. This may sound a bit naive and silly, but I often operate on an *if this were my last day* basis.

If this were my last day, means this is as rich as I ever get to be, as enlightened as I'm ever going to be, as at peace as I can ever be, as compassionate and understanding as I'm capable of being, as loved by another as I can be and so on. Then what's there really to think about? What to cook for dinner? What kind of snowman to build with the girls? What TV show to watch before bed once my wife and I have finally gotten the girls to sleep and hung up the laundry?

Responsibility when seen through the lens of a single day is remarkably straightforward. In fact, in hindsight, the burden of oppression I'd felt was because I had been taking responsibility for things where it was not mine to take, while at the same time shirking the responsibilities that were right in front of my face.

I wasn't responsible for my happiness, my peace of mind, my enlightenment, my freedom from suffering or whatever other nonsense I spent all my time obsessing about. I was responsible for cleaning up my room, getting my homework done on time, keeping my promises to my friends, giving my grades my best shot. In fact, had I kept it that simple I would have known then what I know now. That happiness, freedom, peace of mind and so on are simply byproducts of a life that is lived fully. And by 'lived fully', I mean fully *owned*. The good bits and the nasty bits.

Today, I don't believe I'm entitled to absolutely anything more than I have. And I feel grateful for this *one day* I am privileged to enjoy.

Yet, the real paradox is that the more I am willing to adapt myself to life, the more life seems to adapt itself to me. The less I believe I am entitled to, the more I seem to be granted. The more I take care and take responsibility for my own circumstances, the more my circumstances seem to take care and take responsibility for me.

So, to answer your question, after all that: I think awakening is highly overrated. And it is credited with a lot more than it is actually responsible for. Far more powerful than awakening, is the simple and organic process of maturing, which is perpetual. And with maturity comes the realization that suffering is nothing more than an attitude we take towards the vicissitudes of our own life.

Chapter 15
REORIENTATION

Q: I had a powerful awakening experience a few years ago, similar to the one you have described. It has changed my perspective on things. I'm not driven by many of the things that used to get to me. My question is—why do we lose all motivations, interests and social interactions after such an experience? I feel out of phase with society and the people around me. How do you generate motivation in your own life to do things like raise a family or write, for instance?

A: Yes, what you describe is one of the disorienting aspects of awakening. Spiritual writers often paint awakening as a wholly positive experience and fail to address some of its more difficult aspects, such as the loss of motivation and interest in the things that once occupied our attention. Writers who do look at the difficulties, tell us about it in vague and poetic terms which, while having some basis in reality, don't give us a real practical understanding of what we are experiencing.

So, first let's begin with understanding why you are having that awakening experience at all. What is the point of it? Understanding this may help you see why there has been this kind of shift away from interests and motivations for you.

Some fundamental realizations that reveal themselves in awakening (not as an intellectual concept, but as a real and visceral experience) are:

> *Everything appears to be alive and conscious—even so-called inanimate objects.*

The personal self is a mirage, a mental construct of sorts.

Everything including oneself shares a single existence.

My being, your being, the being of a plant or a football is essentially the same being. Everything that exists, exists as a single being.

Life is all there is. Life is god. Life is omnipresent, omnipotent and omniscient. And life has no opposite. There is no such thing as non-life or non-existence.

Once such an awakening has occurred, even if that viewpoint eventually subsides and you find yourself back in your familiar and ordinary perception of self, you will find that the mechanics of your life don't work the way they once did.

Your brain and its reward centres are permanently altered. While you may continue to be able to experience short-term rewards in the form of temporary spikes of good feeling, those experiences are generally short-lived. The kind of satisfaction that pursuing a career or practicing a hobby or listening to music once provided will no longer have the same impact, other than for brief and sporadic intervals of time.

Your self-concept and the ability to construct elaborate narratives of a self will also be impaired. This means that the concept of becoming a 'somebody' will no longer drive you with the consistent power which drives most people around. Again, this will come in fits and starts, but will fail to convert into any real momentum.

With no identity to build upon and no real passionate purpose to drive you, you might imagine the kind of bizarre limbo this represents. In your case, though, you needn't imagine it, you're living it! What follows is what I sometimes refer to as a 'vacuum phase'. It's like the feeling of losing a loved one or a career in which you have invested your whole life. This vacuum phase is really a grieving period. One in which the brain is slowly catching up to the fact that life is different now and all the things that once preoccupied it are no longer relevant. It takes time for that to sink in and process.

Again, much of the contemporary spiritual literature does nothing to orient us to this new reality. The emphasis on life after awakening as all love and light and full of passionate purpose is not helpful. All such self-help, motivational verbiage does is to keep us stuck in a fear and lack-based mindset.

So, to return to the question: What is the point of awakening? The point is to reorient you. To set you in an altogether different direction.

Many people live what I call an object-oriented existence. Their entire existence is preoccupied with perceiving everything, including themselves, as objects. Life then becomes about how to interact with, attract, avoid, enhance, negate, destroy or create objects. By 'objects' I refer not only to physical bodies but to experiences and events as well. Marriage, career, finances, sports, hobbies—and even spirituality in this sort of mindset—are all seen as objects to possess or acquire. The ultimate object being the self-identity, which is enhanced. And the self is enhanced by procuring and enhancing as many of the other objects as possible.

When we have an awakening we realize that there are no such objects 'out there,' or at least not in the sense we once believed. Separation and independent existence are only apparent. There is something much more fundamental linking everything and encompassing it and that is *being*. Awakening is that shift from an object-oriented existence to a *being*-oriented existence.

As I mentioned earlier, it can take a brain a long time to catch up to the fact that not only has such a shift occurred but that everything has become oriented in a wholly different direction. It may continue to try and follow old patterns of seeking to enhance itself by focusing on objects. But all that falls flat in the end. The boat is sailing the other way. This is why objects themselves—whether in the form of careers we once had, hobbies we once pursued, music we once loved, or sports we were once passionate about—fail to generate anything more than a passing enthusiasm.

Those objects ceased to be the point the moment that awakening happened. It's just that your brain failed to get the memo.

Everything becomes oriented to encourage the brain's perspective to shift away from objects to the dimension of *being* underlying these objects. To experience *being* we are required to be centred in the present. *Being* is the only thing our minds cannot abstract into imagination. Objects, on the other hand, can be rendered abstract, even in their absence using 'objectives'. *Being,* on the other hand, cannot be pursued in this manner. It can only be experienced in the form of whatever object appears in the moment.

In that vein, *being* becomes paramount above all else. Above careers, above relationships, above hobbies or life goals. We are therefore becoming oriented into a way of living that may have been unfathomable to us previously.

You asked me what motivates me now: to write, to take part in my family life and so on. My only motivation is the 'thread of *being*'. I follow that thread and allow it to unfold my life for me. I don't write because I 'choose to'. Following the thread of *being* I come upon an inspiration and that inspiration leads me to write. Similarly, following the thread of *being* I come upon love for my wife and a bottomless well of adoration for my kids. And I follow that love and adoration and it inspires dedication and devotion in me.

This is not a one-time thing. It is a moment by moment experience. I come upon that inspiration to write repeatedly anew. I come upon that love and adoration repeatedly and anew. And if one day, following the thread, I were to no longer encounter that inspiration then I simply wouldn't write. I would do whatever the moment required. And if following the thread, I found I no longer came upon the love and adoration, then I would follow that thread wherever it took me. There is no judgment here. Nor any moral pedestal that dictates down to me. *Being* is paramount and parsing that thread is my sole purpose.

And strangely, I have found that even though this sounds like a recipe for chaos and hedonism (as anyone living in an object-oriented existence may project, and perhaps for them it may actually turn out that way if they tried to operate similarly) it has actually led to a greater and more exquisite order in my life than my personality could ever have managed. I, for one, once believed myself incapable of being in a committed long-term relationship and especially being a decent parent to children. And yet, by simply following that thread of *being*, all that has unfolded effortlessly. By not making marriage and parenting into goals and objectives, they have flowered miraculously and enhanced my life in ways I could never have even dreamed.

And the best thing is I feel no sense of personal achievement about any of it whatsoever. Only a sense of profound gratitude.

The same is true for writing.

The object-oriented life is like the salmon swimming upstream. Such a salmon is driven by a force of desperation to somehow return to its origins. It does this by treating the river as a hostile adversary that must be struggled against and overcome. Progressing 'upwards', up the mountain, many perish. A few make it to their destination, upon which they spawn and promptly die.

However, picture the salmon who at a certain point in the struggle is hit by a strong current out of nowhere and suddenly finds itself facing downstream. For a while this salmon will thrash about. It will lament the fact that other salmon are passing it by quickly while it feels stuck and unable to move in that direction in a meaningful way.

Eventually, that salmon will give up fighting. When it does it will find that there is a whole different way of living. All it needs is to follow the current of the river. And the river provides what it needs.

And while the salmon may not fully realize it, its final destination is not some breeding ground where it is destined to perish. Rather it is the ocean of experience into which all rivers feed. The source of life itself.

Chapter 16

LAW OF INERTIA

My critique of organized meditation in the essay titled 'Where all Paths Lead', as a superior form of spiritual practice, generated quite a bit of debate both on and offline. This is only to be expected. It was like walking into a bodybuilding gym and telling people that lifting weights isn't a particularly great way to get fit. In the so-called "spiritual community" meditation practice is seen as an undisputed means to achieving spiritual insight, enlightenment or progress of some unspecified kind.

At the very least, meditation is seen as a means of developing mental health: a balanced state of mind in which thoughts, emotions and actions all harmonize into a seamless flow. Meditation is supposed to make us peaceful, wise, non-reactive, compassionate and a whole slew of very, very desirable personality traits. While meditation certainly has some psychological benefits, it is by no means a magic wand using which all problems can be banished. However, it does have a useful function as a broom to sweep all our problems under the rug.

But first an aside about inertia.

Resistance to Change

Newton's first law of motion[20] states that *a body at rest will continue to be at rest and a body in motion will continue to remain in motion unless acted upon by an external force.*

---

20. The three laws of motion were first compiled by Isaac Newton in his *Philosophiæ Naturalis Principia Mathematica* (Mathematical Principles of Natural Philosophy), published in 1687.

The same is true of a mind.

In fact inertia is, most simply put, a resistance to change.

Why do most people even embark on a spiritual path or take up a meditation practice? It's because they feel utterly wasted by the momentum of their minds. They feel as if they are on a runaway train over which they have little to no control. Many of us have struggled with the inertia of the mind's momentum. It generates anxiety, paranoia, stress, depression, fear, anger and, in some cases, a desire to simply self-destruct in order to put an end to the madness.

When someone who feels like this begins a meditation practice, the effects can be quite beneficial. In this case meditation acts as an antidote for the inertia of the mind's momentum. It acts as the Newtonian external force, influencing the mind to shift from a state of movement to a state of rest.

Let's say someone is a workaholic and is completely burnt out—some time off to rest and recuperate may be just what they require. Or if someone is physically exhausted from a day of hard labor, then sitting on a couch and doing absolutely nothing may be just what they need to rejuvenate.

At a certain point the couch-sitting starts becoming counterproductive. In a case of diminishing returns, there is a certain point in which the balance switches and what was a solution becomes a problem. The hard worker turns into a couch potato and is now incapable of generating any energy whatsoever to get up and do any work.

The inertia of momentum has simply been replaced by the inertia of rest. And just as an external force was needed to shift the body from movement into rest, an external force will now be required to shift it from rest into movement.

This is what happens to many 'spiritual' people: people who feel that all solutions to the problem of existence can be found, just by meditating. After a while these individuals find that they begin to lack in motivation, then desire, then any real passion or interest and finally they lack any real emotion. Being at rest for so long, the mind turns into a couch potato. And then it sort of settles into its own ass-groove.

Now, a person like this may claim not to be suffering in the same sense that others—those dominated by the inertia of momentum—are suffering. But that's like a guy sitting on the couch all day who may claim that he doesn't get injured at work like the other guys working on construction sites. He doesn't realize that his inaction and lethargy are causing another form of injury to his body. Similarly, many spiritual folk, stuck in a mindset of *'there's nothing to do because there is "no doer" who is doing it'* end up suffering in a whole different way: from a lack of any real spark or vitality in their day to day life.

Spiritual Denial

Rest is the antidote to too much action. Action is the antidote to too much rest. To quote Newton's Third Law, 'every action has an equal and opposite reaction' and those who fail to understand this end up getting stuck on one end of the spectrum or the other.

A body must be allowed to do what a body is designed to do. Similarly, a mind must be allowed to do what a mind is designed to do. And that is to think! Thoughts are treated as such a taboo in some parts of the spiritual community that not thinking is considered the pinnacle of spiritual achievement. How utterly idiotic! That would be like some guy sitting on the couch claiming to have reached the pinnacle of health by virtue of the fact that he hasn't lifted a finger all day.

Thinking is what the mind is designed to do. And a mind that is afraid to think is going to seed. Perhaps, because of the obsessive-compulsive nature that our minds have developed in a society that places an overemphasis on the analytical information-processing type of thinking, we come out of it feeling all too spent. And because of that experience we vow never to return to that hell again.

So, we find a nice breezy spot within our minds, where we camp out. Initially the silence and the calm feel extremely therapeutic. Yet, over time we find ourselves wanting to stay there more and more, not because it feels so good, but because we are terrified of ever leaving.

As a resident of an apartment building that is on fire may move to the rooftop terrace to get some fresh air and escape the smoke and flames, we retreat into meditative silence as a means of gasping for some fresh air. Yet, after some time in this elevated head-space of inner calm and mental placidity, we may actually begin to convince ourselves that the building isn't on fire anymore. Sitting on the terrace of our own consciousness we convince ourselves that nothing is the matter. Or better yet, the building underneath us isn't *really* our home.

But those flames aren't going anywhere. Sitting on the rooftop certainly is not doing anything to put them out. And, over time, the flames will find their way up to the roof as well. That's simply the nature of fire.

What's the solution? For me it was realizing that I had to go back into the fire. Retreat as often as I may need to for a gasp of fresh air, but don't linger.

What most people call spiritual practices are really psychological techniques. By using them we compartmentalize our pain and store it away: out of sight and out of mind. There is a difference between surfacing on the rooftop for fresh air and actually living there. The deep denial of their own angst, where most people in the spiritual community live, is tragic and pathetic.

We see it online all the time: people almost tripping over one another to shower each other with hearticons, *namastes* and blessings, professing universal love at the drop of a hat. And yet, at the smallest sign of disagreement they turn vicious—ripping each other to shreds over the pettiest of arguments. A psyche whose primary preoccupation is denial of its own fractures and weaknesses is bound to be fragile and thereby perpetually defensive.

Own up

The highest form of spiritual practice that I have ever found is not meditation or any such mechanical activity. It is *taking responsibility* for myself. That includes actions, emotions, thoughts and intentions. Recognizing that, for each one of us, the buck ultimately stops right here, with oneself.

No one else can take responsibility for the shit we find ourselves in, nor is anyone to blame. To stand on my own feet means not using another human being, object or ideology as a crutch (or scapegoat!). What could be more spiritual than to take full responsibility for oneself? To take all the power that was given away to external authorities: people, governments, spiritual texts, gurus and concentrate it within. To claim sole authority in my own life. Is there anything more empowering than that?

Someone asked me recently what kind of spiritual practice I recommend as the best. I'll tell you what mine is: it's simply being absolutely present with myself no matter what I'm doing. I own the experience. I take full responsibility. If I'm thinking, then I'm thinking full out. If I'm watching tv, then I'm watching tv, all in. If I'm shoveling the snow, then I'm shoveling the snow like it's my last chance to shovel snow.

What there isn't, is that voice in my head going: *is this what I should be doing?* I bludgeoned that question to death with an axe years ago. I am the sole authority on myself. Who the fuck is going to be telling me what I *should* do?

Yet, taking responsibility also means that we are aware of consequences and hold ourselves fully responsible for what happens as well. If I run a red light going, *who the fuck is going to tell me what I should do?* Then I'm an idiot. The fact is there are rules that I have willingly agreed to and, in agreeing to them, I have accepted certain outcomes of breaking those rules. Yet, none of this disempowers me.

There's talk about not relying on outer authorities that gets tossed around, but few people understand what that actually means. It means being adrift in the ocean without a lifeline, it means getting used to uncertainty as a constant companion, it means walking through dark woods without a map. It's much easier said than done. Everyone wants the kind of freedom that comes with that romantic notion of being free from the dictates of others. They don't realize how much security those kinds of dictates actually bring to our life. Traversing life without any real external coordinates is a hell of its own. And yet, for those who are determined to orient that way, it's the only way worth living.

Not Silence, Flow. Not Action, Flow.

Tormented by the inertia of the mind's momentum, we trade it in for the inertia of mental inaction. But that produces its own kind of torment. The real key lies in the transition. The ability to shift from one to the other when the need feels appropriate. It lies in the ability to overcome one's own inertia.

What does the moment of transition feel like? What does the experience of overcoming inertia feel like? It feels like *resistance*.

A ball is rolling and you slow it down with your hand. The experiencing of bringing that ball to rest is one of resistance. Similarly, you give the ball a little push to get it moving. Once again, the weight of the ball, as you get it going, feels like resistance.

We have come to believe erroneously that the feeling of

inner resistance is a negative and undesirable one. And so, we convince ourselves that as long as there is no resistance there is no problem. In fact, this sentiment is unanimously adopted by people from all walks of life. The only reason why our first-world societies can perpetuate these paradigms of mass consumption and consumerism is because we have come to believe that convenience is the highest virtue. In other words, anything that makes life easier must be good for us.

Inertia is easy street. Just keep doing what you're doing and hope it all works out. This kind of life requires absolutely no intuition and a minimum of intellect to perpetuate.

As long as we continue to uphold spiritual values that promote ease, calm and peace as the highest virtues and any form of resistance or turmoil as bad and to be avoided at all cost, then we just continue to perpetuate the same models of consumerism and convenience that society is perpetuating. We are spiritual consumerists, desperately seeking to avoid the harsh realities of life by creating bubbles of psychological security surrounded by every source of feel-good emotion one could want, within which we hope to live out the rest of our lives.

And while we may convince ourselves that the lives we are living are based upon a deep and profound truth, in reality we are no less shallow, superficial and self-absorbed than the rest.

Resistance is key, it's crucial because it reveals absolutely everything. And to learn how it works we must become actively interested in our own resistances. Let us be willing to explore. To enter the burning building and investigate the source of the flames.

When learning to drive a manual transmission in a gas fuelled car: shifting gears is one of the most challenging aspects of driving. Especially, for someone who has learned to drive only an automatic transmission, the desire to just let the gearbox be and drive on the same single gear is strong. But if you rev too hard on the first gear you will overheat your engine. And if you drive too slow on fifth you will stall it.

A perpetually moving mind is like a car that is red lining[21] because it is stuck in first gear. A mind clinging to the meditative state is like a car stalling in fifth. An unwillingness to learn that gears need to shift at different speeds is not going help you drive that car any better. In fact, it's only when we truly learn to enjoy the resistance that gears provide that we learn how to transition more effortlessly from one state to the next.

In the beginning, we may need mechanical cues such as watching the RPMs[22] in order to know when to shift. But over time, one begins to get a feel for it. Hard and fast rules for shifting may work on flat terrain, but as the terrain becomes hilly, the rules for shifting change with elevation. Without a feel for the gearbox, we will not achieve effortless, comfortable and efficient driving.

With enough practice, we can develop the ability to do all kinds of things like double-shifting and downshifting around curves that not only increase the quality of the drive but make it increasingly enjoyable.

Similarly, in order to get a real feel for our own minds, we need to be willing to explore and work with its resistances. Shifting from rest to movement, accelerating and decelerating at will, may seem like an impossible task for someone who has only learned to drive on an automatic transmission. But that is the only way to take responsibility of one's own mind. It's the only way to fully own its architecture and to use it and enjoy it the way it was designed to **be.**

At a certain point the transitions become second nature. Then driving becomes automatic in a wholly different sense.

21. Red lining: the indicator on a car's dashboard shows goes to red, telling the driver that he/she is exceeding the maximum engine speed at which an internal combustion engine can operate without causing permanent damage.

22. RPMs: Revolutions per minute in a gas/petrol fuelled car engine. Each gear should operate only between a certain level of RPMs.

That is when car and driver cease to be separate but become one seamless flow. The mind ceases to be an alien creature to be avoided, silenced, denied or dominated. It becomes integrated as an inseparable part of the whole.

That, to me, is the real purpose of spiritual practice.

Chapter 17
NO COMPROMISE

I am fundamentally unable to see even a smidgen of authority in anyone or any institution outside of myself and my own existence.

This wasn't always the case. For the greater part of my life I honestly believed there were those who knew better, who were more qualified, who had a superior understanding of this thing we call *life* than I did. But now, that's utter nonsense to me.

I once held the likes of Ramana Maharshi and Nisargadatta in great reverence. I once had great admiration for teachers like J.Krishnamurti and Alan Watts. I was filled by a longing for the saintliness of a Yogananda or a Ramakrishna Paramahamsa. I was mesmerized by the mystical otherworldly gaze of an Osho or an Anandamayi Ma. I marvelled at the austerity of Himalayan sadhus. I was humbled by the simplicity of the Zen monks. My heart felt warmed to the point of tears by the goodness of the Dalai Lama or Mother Teresa.

And now in hindsight, all I can say is: *What the fuck was I thinking?*

Of course, I know only too well what I was thinking then, so the question is rhetorical. But that my perspective could have been so warped, so as to believe that another human being could assume such value that I would place them even a fraction of a millimeter above myself, is something that blows my mind.

Rámana, some kid who ran away from home and sat in some cave. What twists our minds into believing that he has absolutely anything of worth to offer? Nisargadatta, a bidi seller in the slums of Mumbai—who gives a shit what he has to say about the "absolute"? The Dalai Lama, just some child upon whom some superstitious title of power and influence from some archaic tradition was thrust? Who the hell made him a 'somebody' in my world?

Don't get me wrong. These are all charismatic individuals, some of them born to command an audience, many of them brilliant thinkers, a few of them deep meditators and mystics. So they got skills. So what? Watching Michael Jordan slam dunk a basketball sure as hell isn't going to make me able to jump like him. Watching a pimply kid take some class project and turn it into the most successful social media company of all time isn't going to make me become one of the eight most wealthy people in the world. So, why do I care for what ego death this Ramana dude claims he had in his bedroom at the age of fifteen?

Of course, I gave *so so so* many fucks once upon a time. But now it all seems kind of perverse. To give one iota of credence, to what another person is experiencing over what I am experiencing, feels like a betrayal of the deepest kind. It is tantamount to spiritual desertion.

I don't care if I'm the most unenlightened shmuck to have ever existed on the planet. But at least that is *my* experience. It is real. However daft my perspective, at least it is what I *see*. It is what *is*. I don't care if the Buddha has Nirvikalpa Samadhied up the yin yang, what is *real* is that I experience what I experience.

To trade even a moment of that, for the pseudo-experience of someone who is having a better moment feels like the most ungrateful thing I could ever do. It would feel like I've sold myself out. Like I just threw myself under the bus. I couldn't look at myself in the mirror. All I would see is a sellout.

All of us, who either in the past or the present, flocked from one teacher to another. All of us who listened to this person's words or that person's. All of us who spoke praises of the awakened perspective of this dude sitting on a special chair. There is only one word that describes what we are: *groupies*.

No different than any other groupie trying to sneak backstage and party with the band. Where is the self respect?

No compromise.

There cannot be any compromise on this single moment we have been gifted. It's not worth trading it in for the promise of great riches, great luck, great knowledge, great love or great realization. The two dollars and fifty cents in your pocket is worth infinitely *more to you* than the billions Mark Zuckerberg has in the bank. The bumpy road you've travelled on and the few hard knock lessons you've learned are profoundly more valuable *to you* than the wisdom of all the sages in the world. The struggles in your relationships and the communication challenges you work at with your significant other or your kids are leaps and bounds more substantial than the words of the greatest relationship gurus and self-help experts out there.

In short, the lives of other people are nothing more than *entertainment*. It's a reality show. It's real to *them*, not to you. What's real to you is what's happening right now. Not the abstract meanderings of some dead Indian dude whom you've never met.

And yet, we sell out. We compromise. Again and again, we compromise. Not realizing that each time we do, we die a little death. Because that is essentially what happens when you trade one moment away for the promise of another one. Something inside feels deeply betrayed. Deeply shamed. Deeply alone and isolated. Deeply unworthy.

It's not rocket science. It really isn't. It's so simple. *This* is what we've got. *This* is the ride we are on. And *this* step we are taking is all that matters. Even if it looks like chopping vegetables. Even if it looks like trying to pass a painful kidney stone that feels like the size of a ping-pong ball.

Honor it. Honor yourself. Own it. Don't trade it away for some moment some other fucker has already happily enjoyed and is dangling in front of your foolish face like a carrot.

The promise is the curse. The hope is the despair. Eternal life is dying a slow death moment after moment after moment.

No compromise. Be you. Do you. Exclusively to no exception. Fuck what someone else is doing, feeling or experiencing. It's none of your business.

This is reality. Not a reality show.

Chapter 18

BALANCE OF POWER

Q: I have only experienced a few flashes over the years, but it seems like the same things have gradually fallen away. Gave up on the idea of 'waking up naked and laughing on my kitchen floor'. Guess I'm on the slow train….

A: There is this invisible barrier within the world of so-called 'spirituality' between the haves and the have-nots. Just as in any other aspect of life this is how division is made and power is consolidated. There are the wealthy and the rest who struggle to pay bills. There are the famous and the rest of us who live in obscurity. There are those who have found their passionate purpose and others who are stumbling through their lives. There are those who have found that soulmate and the rest who are bumbling through one unfulfilling relationship to the next.

The have and have-not dynamic exists in practically every aspect of life you can imagine. So, why should spirituality be exempt?

Here those who have had the so-called "awakening experience" are set apart in a class by themselves. They're the ones who have hit the jackpot on the spiritual slot machine we've been sitting at and cranking away on a daily basis. We want to hear the *ching, ching, ching* as hundreds of coins of insight come cascading down upon us in a deluge. We want to be sitting naked on the kitchen floor and laughing…

The goal of a *have-not* is to be a *have* and the goal of a *have* is to try and maintain the status quo. Because unless a certain critical mass of have-nots is maintained, the entire power structure can flip over.

So, let me start by first saying: it's all bullshit. There is always going to be some aspect of life in which you are a *have*. There are always also going to be many aspects of life in which you are the *have-not*. And chances are the *have-not* slice of the pie is going to be significantly larger that the *have*-slice. This is generally how it is for pretty much everyone you meet. I don't care if you're a Dalai Lama or a Mark Zuckerberg.

Secondly, having something doesn't increase a person's power, it only creates the *illusion* of power in the minds of those who don't have that specific thing. We project power onto others in the context and proportion in which we ourselves feel it lacking. It is the intensity of lack and the powerlessness that we feel towards this lack that we then translate into the power we see in someone else.

Several years ago, I attended a Romanian wedding in Bucharest. At the reception, as the first course of appetizers arrived, I hungrily ate everything on my plate. At a certain point I noticed others at the table looking at me with a strange glance. I asked my wife if there was something wrong and she laughed, "you need to pace yourself."

"Why?"

"You have no idea how much food is still coming."

I scoffed at her comment. I've always prided myself on my appetite and my ability to eat an obscene amount of food if necessary. But what I wasn't prepared for was the number of courses yet to come. Starting at 7pm, every hour on the hour, we were served another course. Cabbage rolls, then steak, then chicken, then salmon fillet, then sausage, then…it went on and on. The final course was served at 2:00 am. And *that's* when the dessert courses began…

My mind was simply struggling to compute the insanely copious amounts of food being brought out. Entire plates were being sent back untouched by the guests and still the food kept coming. I asked a friend why this was happening. Why this crazy amount of food when no one was eating it at all. And he remarked,

"We lived in poverty for so long and finding food was such a struggle that serving these kinds of feasts, even today, is seen as a mark of power and stature."

Now, those who have grown up in more affluent societies would not be impressed with this sort of display, we'd find it wasteful and abhorrent. But within a psyche that has faced deprivation for so long this is exactly the sort of extravagant display that embodies power. If I were a Romanian farmer struggling to put food on the plate, a man who could serve limitless courses of food through the night would certainly be someone worthy of respect and even worship in my eyes.

So, let's understand that the value we ascribe to experiences, especially the ones we are really hankering for, have less to do with the experiences themselves and everything to do with the intensity of our hankering, as well as the degree of deprivation we are experiencing.

Now… let me return to the topic of awakening.

In the chapter entitled "Orientation", the questioner's query was a specific one. As someone who had experienced an awakening, he was struggling to reorient himself to his new reality. And so, my response was designed to address his specific query, but this by no means implies that awakening is the only cause of such a reorientation.

Awakening is simply one avenue *by which such a reorientation happens.*

All kinds of experiences can cause you or me to reorient. There are people I know who have gone through the loss of loved ones, multiple divorces, failures in business, physical disability and so on who then emerge from these experiences much more naturally aligned with the flow of life and with far less inner resistance of the ego. They have a natural wisdom and ease about them, even if they may not be able to put it into words philosophically like so many of us do. These people have never had an "awakening" of the spiritual or mystical kind. But their experiences have served as a wake-up call, nonetheless.

There are also those who go through all kinds of mystical, even supernatural, experiences that have the same effect of reorientation. There are those who have had near-death experiences, out-of-body experiences, drug induced visions and so on, who also then find themselves fundamentally altered in how they view themselves in relationship to life. Now, I am not going to discuss the validity or invalidity of these sorts of mystical experiences here. I am simply pointing to the fact that, whether real or not, the net effect seems to be one of a fundamental shift.

Even the examples I've given above merely outline a special subset of experiences that cause this kind of reorientation, by which I mean sudden and unexpected experiences. But there are many cases in which there has been no sudden ground-breaking experience of any sort. There is only a gradual shifting of perspective that happens almost indiscernibly over a long period of time. And still, the net effect is the same.

It all depends on the individual. I may be in a career ill-suited for me that is actively causing me harm, eroding my confidence, compromising my relationships and so forth. But I am too identified with my role within the organization. In this case, nothing short of a sudden event, where I am let go of against my own will, will serve to reorient me towards a line of work more suited to my aptitudes. Another employee may not need to be fired in order to make this career shift. They may gradually, through reflection, come to realize the same thing and simply quit and find a new line of work. Two different solutions for two different sorts of employees.

It seems to me that the kinds of experiences we have that reorient us are the kinds of experiences we need. In hindsight,

I can see that, given the makeup of my mind and how deeply entrenched my sense of identity was in an almost pathological sense of suffering, (I actually took pride in my own suffering) nothing short of a complete zap of lightning would have shifted me off that path.

I have known others close to me, who in believing life to be a process they can control through amassing wealth, power and status, have constantly had experiences of deep loss occur over and over again in the most bizarre ways. And only by having that rug of control pulled out from under them have they gradually learned to relinquish control.

Awakening, thus, isn't a one-size-fits-all solution to one's existential dilemmas. It is a specific prescription for a very specific ailment. If you haven't received that prescription, it may just mean that those are not the symptoms you are suffering from.

However, rest assured that you *are* being reoriented. It may not happen the way it happened for me and some others but what does that matter? Imagine a person suffering from stomach cramps complaining that all they get is two boring pills every day instead of the cool shot of morphine that the guy with the broken arm is given. Not to mention the wicked cool cast that all his friends and family get to autograph.

This exact sentiment is the premise of the famous Nobel Prize for Literature winning novel, *The Magic Mountain,* by the German author Thomas Mann. The plot revolves around a sanatorium in the Swiss Alps where people with all sorts of illnesses go to rest and be treated for their symptoms. Each of these characters uses their own illness as a sort of badge of honor by which to elevate themselves over the others. Believing that their own suffering is of the highest and noblest order they feel superior by virtue of their ailment. I've often felt the spiritual community and the culture it promotes is a spitting image of this book.

Yet, while all the other characters are embroiled in their games of suffering one-upmanship, the protagonist, a young boy named Hans is able to see the real value and truth underlying the sanatorium and the suffering that is represented there. What Hans comes to realize is that one must go through the experience of deep sickness and death to arrive at a higher sanity and health.

There are 7.5 billion sick people on this planet in various stages of recovery. And each is encountering the kind of experiences that are designed to eventually bring them to that *higher sanity and health*. That process will differ for each person. Sometimes it may seem entirely counterproductive. Sometimes it may seem like nothing is happening at all. Sometimes it may seem like fireworks. But it isn't for us to judge. We lack the necessary vision to grasp this completely.

Awakening is a potent experience, but it isn't this golden egg that it's cracked up to be.

A misunderstanding of this actually has a counterproductive effect both for those who yearn for it and those who have had it and feel inflated by it.[23] Nowhere is this more apparent than in the codependent guru-disciple dynamics, so rampant in spiritual culture. Awakening reorients the misguided soul by angling them in the right direction. It by no means gives them a hall pass to avoid ever taking any sort of accountability for their own actions. But it is exactly this kind of sensationalization of the awakening experience that skews our perspectives on what has indeed happened.

And thus, the old power dynamics and hierarchies that have plagued us for centuries just reinvent themselves in a new context.

---

23. Inflation: the concept of inflation is explored in Chapter 11, *The Story of the Gamer.*

Chapter 19

SPIRITUAL BULLSHITTERY

Q: With all due respect, I find your approach unnecessarily reductive. I get what you mean about taking responsibility for ourselves. But you also dismiss these age-old spiritual practices and paint all spiritual teachers with the same brush as fraudsters and conmen! Where do you get off making these kinds of claims?

Of course there are some bad apples who take advantage of their students. But there are those who genuinely help as well! I think you are arrogant and lack true discernment. And frankly, you are a hypocrite as well. Aren't you just another spiritual teacher pretending you are not?

A: Yes, it's entirely possible that I'm arrogant and lack true discernment. Unfortunately, there is no way for me to really know that without having true discernment. So, I'm left with the choice of either taking your word for it or my own. For the time being, I'm more comfortable with the latter so that's what I'm going to go with.

Yet you bring up valid questions that deserve reasonable responses (even though the respect you felt was due sort of fizzled out towards the end of your query).

To begin, your summation of what I've said isn't entirely accurate. I haven't said that "all spiritual teachers are frauds and conmen". What I have said is that there are no spiritual "masters". There is a subtle difference between teaching something and claiming mastery in it. "Teacher" is a role whereas "master" is a position of status within a hierarchy—and potentially the pinnacle of the hierarchy, unless we are looking for 'ascended master' status.

In other words, I'm not opposed to people teaching other people things. I'm opposed to power structures that exploit the vulnerable and promote codependent relationships under the guise of helping people.

Now, I've said this before. There was a time when masters were an integral layer of society. Those were the old days in which society existed in strict hierarchies of authority and people were viewed as being unequal. There were masters and slaves, then there were masters and serfs and then there were the masters and the proletariat. But we have supposedly evolved past those societal models a long time ago.

This is why any institution or individual that claims such a status is attempting to reinstate a hierarchy that is no longer relevant. It is no longer congruous with the times. It is a bid to assume authority and control over another individual by subverting that person's autonomy and enhancing one's own stature. And this is something that is common in today's spiritual culture.

Among those claiming to be spiritual teachers only a small percentage are actually teaching at all. Teaching is more than the one-way dissemination of knowledge or information. Most of the individuals calling themselves spiritual teachers are really spiritual preachers.

Teaching involves so much more than that. At the very least, a teacher should have a knowledge of who their students are.

When you think of a schoolteacher, the very least we would expect is that they know the names of each of their students. An excellent teacher is not only inspirational but also cares deeply about the learning and growth of their students. They are thoroughly invested in their students. Even a mediocre teacher will at least make an attempt to try and get to know their students.

Schoolteachers also put in unpaid work in their down time,

creating lesson plans and learning strategies for kids falling behind. They prepare materials, activities, exercises and tests to challenge their students in various ways. While every once in a while, they may have a spur of the moment, spontaneous lesson, even that comes as a result of a lot of background effort.

Many individuals calling themselves spiritual teachers fail to live up to the standard of even the most basic schoolteacher. Many barely know more than a handful of names of the people who spend good money to come and listen to them. Usually it's the names of those who donate the most that get most readily recalled. While they profess deep compassion and love for their students, their real investment in their students' well being and progress seems minimal.

Furthermore, the amount of effort and preparation that goes into the actual lesson is almost laughable. Since everything is supposedly spontaneously arising, meaningful content is often absent. The particularly gifted teachers may have moments of brilliance but even those become woefully regurgitative after a while.

Finally, any teacher, parent or mentor who cares about their ward will look forward in anticipation to the day when the child will outgrow and surpass them.

Student *retention* is not a marker of success, student *turnover* is.

Retention is a marketing strategy. Corporations seek to retain customers. True teachers don't.

I remember meeting my former high school teacher years after graduating who beamed with pride upon hearing that I had procured a job with a top consulting firm straight out of college. My starting salary was probably more than she made after three decades of teaching in India (an injustice of its own which I won't go into here). But the point is there wasn't a hint of envy. Her happiness for me was genuine.

This is a sentiment often absent in spirituality. Students

never surpass teachers. In fact, the greater a student's realization the more proof it becomes of their teacher's superiority! That is the whole reasoning behind the concept of a what is referred to as 'lineage'. Retention is the name of the game here. It is spiritual marketing in the guise of spiritual teaching. You are being bullshitted.

But let's say there are a small subset of individuals who are genuinely interested in their students. They're not in it for the ego boost, the adoration, the power status, the money, the control over others, the sex, the fame and so on. Even this lot, while having good intentions, are somewhat misguided in my opinion. Because what exactly is the subject being taught?

Spirituality? What's that?

If they are involved in teaching some scripture or some spiritual text, then they are simply engaged in propaganda. Dogma and belief systems have little to do with spirituality. And if they are involved with teaching their own philosophy of life, then that is another form of propaganda.

Spirituality quite simply isn't something one can teach. It isn't a set of rules or mechanism or model or code of conduct. It is the highly personal experience of existing. And how can something like that be taught? Can anyone teach you how to exist? No, we all exist in equal measure. Someone may help you enjoy the process a bit better. But that has nothing to do with spirituality.

So, while there may be some well-intentioned folks out there teaching spirituality to others, I think they're likely just as clueless as the ones they're teaching. They are bullshitting themselves. In fact, individuals with real insight would outright reject such a preposterous title.

Through my writing I offer an example by which others may find relevant insights into their own existence. Rather than templates, I provide samples from my own experience that others can freely choose to relate to, or reject, as they see fit. There is no teaching, there is no knowledge being imparted.

I write about my life, my experience and the understandings and insights that have emerged from that. In short, I share my own highly personal experience of existing: *my* spirituality. And that, in my opinion, is as much as anyone can offer.

The rest is just blatant consumerism in which you are the very product you are being charged to purchase. You are the very service you are being duped into subscribing to.

I'd much sooner choke on a gallon of snake oil.

Chapter 20

WHAT ARE YOU?

Q: You seem comfortable being yourself. To be honest, I envy you. This is like the holy grail for me. I never felt comfortable being myself. The only way of being for me is constant anxiety that turns into panic. My only goal is to somehow change that. I don't want to feel like this anymore. There were a few times when that anxiety suddenly disappeared. It happened a few times during meditation. I experienced Pure Awareness. It was clear that there is no one here. No doer is actually doing any of this. It was the most peaceful I ever felt. Now all I can think is how can I get back there. It's the only experience of living without this suffering "me". I'm tired of this person.

What is your experience of life now? Do you experience no doership? Are you pure awareness?

A: In 1992, at the age of eleven, I moved to Mumbai from Kolkata. It was December and we were staying at a temporary apartment while waiting for our permanent home to be arranged. My father had a chauffeured car, that the bank he worked for had organized. The chauffeur was a middle-aged Muslim man named Latif.

Every morning Latif would pick me up from home and take me to school and in the afternoons, when the school day ended, would bring me back home again. He was a kindly man whose hair was dyed red with henna. He had a soft spot for me and would affectionately call me "Baba".

One afternoon, as the school day ended I went outside to find Latif waiting for me. He looked nervous and distracted. His white trousers were stained red in places.

'Kya hua, Latif?' (What happened, Latif?) I asked.

'Baba,' he said, his voice quivering, 'Sab ekdum paagal ho gaye…' (Everyone's gone insane…)

I looked inside the car to see the back seat streaked with blood.

December 1992, was when the Mumbai riots between Hindu and Islamic political factions began and lasted for nearly two months. During this period the city was a war zone. Prominent buildings were bombed, a mosque was set on fire. Cars, buses and trucks lay overturned and blazing. Innocent people —even women and children—were being hacked to death by the bloodthirsty sword wielding Hindu and Muslim mobs.

'Aaj tum mussalman ho, samjhe!' Latif said to me in the sternest voice I'd ever heard from him (Today you are a Muslim, understand?)

I nodded. The route we would be taking was through a predominantly Muslim residential area.

In the fevered battle raging in the streets, innocent passersby were being stopped by the religious mobs, from either religion, and asked a single question, 'What are you?! Hindu or Muslim?' Often there was little way to determine what the right answer was. The wrong answer would get you hacked down with a sword.

Fortunately, we made it home that day without being stopped. But the adrenaline surge I experienced on the ride home seared the memory into my mind.

'What are you?!' was the last question many heard before being mercilessly murdered that year. For years I struggled to envision a more absurd way to die.

The Ill-Fitting Suit

I struggle to imagine a more absurd way to live. The thought of answering that question in any definitive way is bizarre to me. The fact that it is so commonplace in everyday life doesn't change my sentiment.

There is always that proverbial sword hanging over our heads to figure out what we are.

Are you a man, a woman? Are you a democrat, a republican? Are you a feminist, a sexist? Are you a snowflake, a pleb? Are you straight, gay? Are you asleep, awake? Are you a sheep, a shepherd? Are you suffering, enlightened? Are you ego, pure awareness?

What are you? is the sword that kills the immediacy of this experience and then butchers it into small, digestible cubes of lifeless verbiage.

The question is everywhere, whether explicitly voiced or silently implied. It is in the eyes of everyone whose gaze you meet: on the train, in the office, at school, at the bank, at the party, at the retreat.

And we are perpetually anxious to answer it, whether by our words, our mannerisms, our attire, our possessions, our body language, our facial expressions. Every ounce of our expression is in active conspiracy to answer this very question.

Because we live in constant fear that if we don't answer that question, that sword will come down upon us.

I know what you are is the sound of ruthless judgment hacking us apart.

You're a loser. You're a terrible mother. You're an entitled brat. You're an ignorant redneck. You're a pervert. You're an unambitious waste of space. You're a bigot. You're a moron. You're a mess. You're so egoic. You're unenlightened. You're not very spiritually advanced. You're a sheep.

It's like wearing a suit with a hundred itchy fibers, poking, scratching and irritating your skin all day long. And your experience of life is one of constant squirming. Trying to get comfortable, just trying: shifting this way, that way, standing, sitting, scratching, itching. All you want to do is tear off the suit.

I get that.

I spent the better part of my life trying to feel comfortable within my own suit. And none of the alterations I tried to make on it worked. Each time, it just felt even more uncomfortable. At a certain point, having failed at improving the experience of living in that suit, I convinced myself that the only solution was to tear it off.

What are you?

What do you mean? There's no one here. There is no one who hears the question and no one who answers it. There is no doer doing anything. There is no-thing here that can be questioned.

If we are paranoid about being found out, invisibility is a tempting delusion.

Then in my twenties, that suit was unceremoniously ripped off me. And for the first time I witnessed life without the chafing fabric of a personality and the restrictive discomfort of a mind. And the freedom of being so utterly naked was incredible.

No more itching, pinching, poking, burning. Just the cool air caressing my skin. I vowed never to wear that suit again. I had finally shed my burden. This was peace. This was freedom.

Yet, over time I felt the suit slipping back on again. I felt the scratch of the fabric and desperately tried taking it off again. No matter how much I tried to shed it, before long, I found myself back in it again.

After that my sole mission was to get back to that place of nakedness. It was the only peace I believed existed. The only freedom.

Inside Out

However, what I would come to realize the hard way, after years of struggle, was that the suit wasn't the problem.

Sure, I could try to shed it and perhaps after trying hard enough I might actually be successful. I could live in that empty, naked state where peace was always apparent. Except, there was something incomplete about that. That sort of freedom felt shallow.

Wasn't I still 'me' whether naked or wearing a suit? Then how could I be truly free if my freedom was dependent on what I was or wasn't wearing? My suit was my humanity, my human mind, my human personality. What kind of life was this if I simply opted out of the human experience altogether?

And so, for the first time I willingly wore the suit. And although it chafed and burned and scratched and scraped, I wore it without complaint. Instead, I allowed myself to observe how I was feeling and let the discomfort be as horribly uncomfortable as it was.

And then one day, I saw it as plain as the light of day. I had been wearing the suit inside-out.

All my life I had seen myself through the outside perspective. The *What are you?!* question had conditioned me to see myself as the image I was showing others. Rather than *me,* I had been experiencing the *image of me* that the world saw. And that image chafed. The outer fabric meant for the world had become the one sitting closest to my skin.

Unlike my awakening (that tearing off of the suit which happened suddenly and without my knowledge) the decision to turn the suit inside-out was a conscious one.

It was a no-brainer. It was simple and utterly obvious.

And once I did that, I ceased to see myself through the eyes of other people. I found that the suit not only fitted, but it was pleasant to wear. It was tailored very specifically for me.

And as relieving as it felt, there was also this urge to kick myself for not having realized this sooner? What was the whole point of suffering such a stupid and pointless error? How sheepish did I feel running around for a lifetime moaning about how uncomfortable I felt when I had been wearing the bloody thing backwards?

It took me some time to understand that there was a point. Now that I have the suit on the right way, I know what the world feels like when they encounter me. I understand the ways in which my personality and mind can jar and cause discomfort to another, how I can scratch and hurt. I also know how warm and comforting that fabric can be. For there were certainly times when it felt good in the past even though those moments were overshadowed by the suffering and complaining.

The suit is like a second skin now, I'm rarely even aware of it. While I do suffer the day to day problems and pains that come with this life, what I no longer suffer is the experience of being myself.

Clothed or unclothed, its all the same to me. And as for the question, *what are you?!*

The only truthful answer I care to give is, *I am what I am.*

Chapter 21
OTHER WORLD

The image is of an elderly man with a long wispy beard. He has the lean and hardened physique of an ascetic. His torso is bare except for a single barely visible thread that crosses diagonally. Below he wears a long saffron cloth which reaches midway down his shins. He stands on the platform of what looks like an ancient and historical structure. His palms are pressed together in prayer his eyes closed in deep absorption. He is engaged in *Surya Namaskar*, 'The Salute to the Sun'. The background is a barely distinguishable sprawling landscape, over-exposed and faded to near white. The sunlight bathes his brown-skinned form and the caption of the Facebook ad reads:

'CNN Create: Discover your spiritual side...'

We often think that belief and ideology are perpetuated by the use of language. But it is remarkable how much of it is created simply with imagery. *A picture is worth a thousand words*, as the saying goes. Nowadays, I am able to perceive just how much propaganda can be generated by a simple and seemingly innocent image. Images are powerful stimulators of the subconscious.

Fifteen or twenty years ago, images like this one would have sent my mind soaring into a euphoric sense of longing for the so called "spiritual" side of myself. It would have inspired me to hop on a plane somewhere or at least quadruple my meditation practice at the time.

I might have rushed off to the bookstore and lost hours of my day in the New Age Spirituality and Philosophy sections. I may have waited for the right book to call out to me. Then, with the book in hand, I would have hurried over to a coffee shop or park somewhere and fawned over its pages. Every few pages, I might have felt a shiver of recognition pass through me and I would have sighed deeply, filled with a bittersweet nostalgic longing for myself. I may have laughed or cried, most likely both at the same time. I most certainly would have glanced up at the people minding their own business around me and been filled with a brimming love for their innocence as well as a sadness for their ignorance. Deep down I would have hoped to catch the eye of a stranger who might know what I know and perhaps then we'd bond in our wordless *knowingness*. Yet most of the people whose eyes I'd catch would likely have averted them because my loving gaze would have looked more like a psycho stare, unbeknownst to me.

I cannot count how many times I have actually lived that scenario. All the places I went searching for my spiritual side —my true self—in bookstores, in coffee shops, in the streets of India or the monasteries of Japan. And every time, driven by this romantic idealism, I felt *him*, my true self, right there, just beyond reach. I could almost touch him, I could smell his scent and I was intoxicated by him....

There is a fundamental difference between spirituality and spiritual romanticism. The former is grounded in reality while the latter is a fantasy-generated construct.

The Romantic Mindset

As a teenager, I thought I knew what love meant. I thought I had it figured out much better than any of the people around me including, and especially, the adults. Of course, I really hadn't the faintest clue. All I had was a body full of raging hormones, deep seated psychological insecurities, emotional neediness and the images society had downloaded into my brain of what love looked like through magazine pictures and soppy movie love scenes.

I was always in search of that person to be "the one". I was looking for that singular moment, when the eyes of two strangers meet and span all of space and time. The love at first sight. And the way I set about trying to get that experience was by replicating what I had been shown. I went to bars and stirred my scotch nonchalantly and would look up suddenly hoping to catch the eyes of my soulmate staring right at me. Never happened. I went to coffee-shops and held my book up pretentiously hoping my soulmate (who was bound to have similar tastes) would come and ask me about it. Never happened. I met and dated people of course and for a while convinced myself that this was love since we were doing all the things they did in the movies—but it always felt empty and in the end fizzled into nothing.

It was only later when I outgrew my romantic notions that I began to really understand what love was about. I fell in love with my best friend of seven years at the time. Love at two thousand and first sight. Today, we have been together for over a decade and I have never loved another person more.

Yet, that love looks absolutely nothing like the love my adolescent self imagined. It isn't glamorous, it's ordinary. It doesn't look like long walks on a beach or vacationing in an exotic country or long nights gazing into each other's eyes and sharing our secrets. Those things happen from time to time but they are not what we live for. Love for us also looks like sleepless nights with kids with stuffy noses. Unending piles of laundry that we tag team and power through while watching our favorite sitcom. Getting over arguments about the bills and then talking through it and holding each other supportively. Love is a sense of, *we are in this together no matter what.* And going to bed grateful for this opportunity we've been given to do this with one another.

Love as seen through the romantic mindset looks nothing like real love. While it is rosy it lacks substance. It is icing with no cake underneath. And while icing may taste sweet, it is the cake that fills the stomach.

The same is true of spirituality.

What is widely considered spirituality[24] by people is nothing more than spiritual romanticism.

The image of the yogi in his Himalayan retreat does for the seeker what the image of a young model in a swimsuit does for the teenage boy. It stimulates fantasy. It creates this otherworldly sensation within us that precipitates a sense of yearning. And what we fantasize as being our 'higher self' is that version of us who lives in this other world.

Yet, that other world is nothing more than the world in our heads. It is a fantasy world.

Spiritual Adolescence

As children, our understanding of the world is fairly straightforward. We believe what we are told is true. Love and authority are often synonymous.

People who have no sense of a spirituality outside of the religious doctrines they have been raised within are, in a sense, spiritual children. Spirituality for these people is externally dictated and prescribed. All they need do is follow the instructions and obediently conform and they will find themselves favored and loved by the deity that they pray to.

There are individuals for whom this sort of framework feels restrictive and contrived. Just as teenagers rebel against the authority of their parents, even risking falling out of favor, and even losing their love, in order to find their own meaning and path, those whom we call seekers are like spiritual adolescents.

24. For a definition of spirituality in the context of this book see 'Introduction'.

They have broken free of the constructs of organized forms of spirituality and are in search of a truer and more meaningful spiritual experience.

Yet, just as most teenagers are filled with romantic and idealistic notions of what the world outside looks like, seekers too are filled with romantic and idealistic fantasies of what spirituality looks like. They are motivated by an intoxicating mixture of hope, frustration, yearning and rebellion and the images of spirituality that they project, which appeal to them, are ones that satiate that electric desire for novelty.

And so spiritual adolescents are drawn to wisdom paths and teachings like teenagers who are drawn to designer clothes and fast cars. They are drawn to gurus and spiritual teachers just as teenagers are drawn to pop stars and celebrities. It is this deep-seated yearning for something infinitely more extraordinary than the ordinary reality around them that keeps their heads craned, their bodies taut and their eyes anticipating.

And just as a youth might bounce from relationship to relationship, believing they have found their soul mate, spiritual adolescents bounce from holy site to holy site, teaching to teaching, believing they have found their spiritual self. But inevitably, the love affair feels short lived. The spiritual self they think they've found seems strangely restricted to a very narrow set of circumstantial conditions.

Their spiritual side feels more like a long-distance relationship that they are always struggling to maintain. Always looking forward to that next retreat, that next gathering, that next trip abroad when they may get to meet their spiritual selves again. Spiritual adolescents are perpetually oscillating between disenchantment and euphoria.

The disenchantment and the euphoria are reactions to two separate realities: this one and the other world in the mind. And as long as the fantasy can be re-created on the outside, the spiritual adolescent feels euphoric and more deeply connected.

But when real life comes crashing back in, disappointment and disconnection ensue.

Nothing Like One Imagines

Fortunately, spirituality is nothing like what we imagine and is everything like what we are. But the good fortune in this statement is not easily grasped. It takes quite a bit of experience, failure and disappointment, the shattering of many fantasies and delusions, before we can even begin to understand what this statement means.

Just as I had to gradually let go of my romantic and vapid notions of love before I was able to see that the soulmate I had been searching for had already been with me, day in and day out, for seven years of my life – so also did I discover that my spiritual side, the true self, that I was always seeking was actually the *whole of me* and had been for the entire time.

And just as I discovered real love was not just the long walks but also the laundry, not just the bedroom conversations but also the bill collection notices, not just sensual baths but also sleepless nights—so also, did I discover that spirituality was simply everything that happens: the good and the bad, the mundane and the extraordinary.

But how do you sell such an idea to someone? How can you sell a life no more significant than the one someone is already living? How do you convince someone to buy something they already have?

You don't. You can't. You simply shouldn't.

What the picture of the old man saluting the sun doesn't reveal is the moment right after; when he steps down from his pedestal and sits atop his bicycle, riding through narrow streets, stopping along the way for the carton of eggs his wife requested him to buy for breakfast that morning only to discover that he has left his wallet behind at home and envisions the terrible scolding he will receive from her if he returns home empty handed (yet again) and so he politely requests the shopkeeper, with whom he is familiar, to put the eggs on his tab and is relieved when the fellow complies and, tucking the eggs under one arm like the precious cargo they are, he rides sheepishly home, thankful for having dodged yet another bullet—and as he does, the sun that he had greeted just moments earlier, now the furthest thing from his mind, continues to light his path home.

Chapter 22
IS THIS ENLIGHTENMENT?

Q: I am writing because I am finding myself in way over my head with this truth-or-death thing I've started.

I will start by saying that a few months ago I fell into what I now believe to have been the void of voids. I was washing dishes, and suddenly life drained out of everything. Everything became ugly. I stopped what I was doing, I was thinking, *No, no, this cannot be, I want to go back!*

I feel there is no point to enlightenment, it's not meant for this world and is totally beside the point. I started this pursuit because I thought I was a dysfunctional person with nothing to lose, but now my dysfunctions are looking pretty good. I feel like I'm in an impossible place. Can't go forward, and don't know if I can go back.

Do you have any words for me? Is this enlightenment?

A: I still remember the day. I was nine years old. I finished my homework rapidly, shoved the entire sandwich my mother had made for me in my mouth, grabbed my cricket bat and went racing out the door. My mother yelled something inaudible as the door slammed shut. I flew down the stairs of the apartment building skipping two steps, then three, then leaping over entire flights at a time. I throttled down the road, turned the corner and then sped through the field to where a group of boys were setting up the wickets.

'Great! You haven't started yet,' I wheezed doubling over to catch my breath.

'Yeah we waited for you, you fucker,' one of the older

boys guffawed.

'Hey, I bet he was busy watching his parents fuck,' his twin brother bellowed as the other boys burst into raucous laughter.

'Fuck you, I wasn't!' I retorted in indignation.

'Don't lie, you shithead. They were busy fucking each other's brains out, weren't they?' More raucous laughter followed.

'You wanna fuck with me?' I was getting angry.

'Ewww, gross!' twin number one chortled.

'Come on buddy! Let's fuck!' I challenged.

'Waitaminute, waitaminute! Do you even know what that word means?' Twin number two was looking at me with an amused expression.

'Of course I do, asshole. It means to fight!' I replied masking my gnawing suspicion that my understanding of the word may have had some holes in it.

'Oh ho ho ho! What we have here boys is one who has yet to be initiated into the dark secrets of life!' Twin two's eyes sparkled mischievously.

What followed over the next ten minutes was my introduction to *Sex talk: the Graphic Novel* version. And the scars it left on my psyche would take many months to heal. For a long time after I could barely look my parents in the eye. They repulsed me. And my own sexual urges repulsed me even more.

I lost my innocence that day and the world turned gray almost overnight. What kind of existence was this where such a disgusting thing had to happen in order for people to be born? Suddenly I saw the parents of all my friends and realized they too had done the nasty. And my grandparents, those sweet, honorable and chaste people had also stripped off their clothes and rolled and howled like animals biting, scratching, screaming, penetrating? Like I said, the boys had painted a pretty picture.

Life began to feel increasingly dirty. And there was nothing I could do about it. I couldn't scrub it off, I was enveloped by it! How does someone swimming in a sewer with no hope of getting out ever get clean? I spent months feeling utterly repulsed by almost everything.

Then one day I came across some romance novels in my mother's room. And I began perusing them out of curiosity. And gradually, I became educated into a whole new way of viewing the sexual act.

These people were not molesting each other on the toilet while I obliviously watched television in the next room (as the twins had vividly illustrated for me). No, they were rolling around in the warm hay of a barn on a stormy night. They were not abusing each other like vermin. No, she was gently grasping his throbbing manhood while he playfully caressed her velvety softness. And as the tip of his tongue rendezvoused with her gently cresting peaks, my revulsion began to give way to the wanton desire to deposit my own fertile loam into the luxuriant delta of another being...

***

Creating narratives, both spectacular and horrific, of the events of our lives as they unfold is something all human beings have a propensity for. It's what, according to the Polish-born philosopher, Alfred Korzybski[25], makes us *time binders*. Civilization as we know it today would not have been possible if this storytelling capacity within us had not been so pronounced. History is, after all, nothing more than the story of humanity.

We create narratives about society, about the world, about other people, about ourselves, about the unknown. So it is unsurprising that all these narratives about what we call 'enlightenment' should exist. The great irony here, of course, is that enlightenment is meant to signify a release from all narratives. But this is just a small inconvenient fact easily swept

25. Montagu, M. F. A. (1953). Time-binding and the concept of culture. The Scientific Monthly, Vol. 77, No. 3 (Sep., 1953), pp. 148–155.

under the rug when we get into it.

And so we end up with a whole spectrum of narratives about what enlightenment is. They range from downright arousing (like two beautiful and amply endowed lovers making passionate love in a barn on a stormy night) to downright terrifying (like imagining your parents writhing in a pile of sweat and stench on the toilet).

Of course, nothing in life is ever that sensational. But we want it to be. We need it to be. Something within us craves sensationalism. It's why tabloid magazines sell better than scientific journals. We want to be shocked, aroused, titillated and terrified—anything to escape the mundane matter-of-factness of this moment as it actually appears.

The shitty (or un-shitty, depending on how you want to see it) reality of the matter is, of course, that nothing can escape the mundane matter-of-factness of this moment. That is all there really is. It's all mundane. It's all matter-of fact.

So you've sprouted angel wings and now can soar high above the city. Well, don't get too pumped about it. This too will become the new normal one day. And when it does, it'll feel like just another boring Monday flying from one ordinary rooftop to the next.

We like to create a great sense of melodrama (positive or negative) about sudden shifts in our perception but really there is nothing either celebratory or distressing about any of it. It's a natural aspect of how all beings evolve. Only we tend to react in these ways because we are used to blowing things out of proportion.

For instance, calling what you experienced 'falling into the void of voids' is unhelpful language, in my opinion. It makes you sound like Daenerys Targaryen[26] venturing into the mouth of hell to become the Mother of Dragons. It makes for an entertaining narrative but that's about it.

26. From *Game of Thrones*, TV series.

So you had an epiphany. Ok. So you realized the world is ugly and that even loved ones can be vile and despicable. No problem. Hell, my kids are vile and despicable several times a day. They are inspiring and adorable as well. I am vile and despicable as fuck sometimes and it's a wonder anyone puts up with me. So what? None of this represents the absolute state of things. You have finally seen that all human beings are lovable creatures who are equally detestable at the same time. We are every bit as worthy of being disliked as we are of being liked.

This is what sobering up looks like. If getting sober was easy, every addict would be doing it. There is a reason they're not. And that's because the addict realizes that getting sober doesn't make our issues go away. It just makes them all the more starkly apparent.

To me, enlightenment is not some pinnacle state of consciousness but rather is a continuous process of ever-increasing clarity about self and reality—a process that every sentient being is involved in, whether we are aware of it or not. And this process contains revelations which feel earth-shattering when they happen, yet in hindsight we see them as nothing more than a casual step forward. It's not a change in perception that's worth singing praises off the peak of some mountain over. Nor is it something worth screaming in horror over, as if you've just seen a killer clown in a sewer. You are being gradually stripped of your cozy black and white way of viewing things and are instead being immersed in a mandala of infinite grays.

It takes a little bit of time to reorient to this new normal. But it'll happen just as it always has. It's more like the memory of being dumped by your high school sweetheart. At the time it was agonising and you believed at the time that you would never recover from the pain. The loss of the rose-tinted view often feels as if the color has drained from your life. But in time the clarity gained is something far more fulfilling and a rewarding part of the journey to maturity.

This revelation feels so burdensome right now because it is being loaded with significance and seriousness. It isn't actually all that serious a matter. As you are experiencing the crisis of the decade, your body is still carrying on as usual, the birds are still going about their business, couples across the world are still making love in a variety of locations and the business of life goes on as usual.

So my first suggestion to you would be, no matter how profound of a shift in view you think you've had, lighten up about it. Give it time and try not to get ahead of yourself. None of it is a big deal.

The most exciting part of your revelation, as far as I'm concerned, was the part when you said,

'I was washing the dishes.'

Chapter 23
SHORT AND SWEET

Someone recently commented after reading some of my articles that I was 'not one for brevity'. So, I've decided to keep this one short and sweet…

In less than 80 years from now (approximately the same amount of time since WWII began) you will probably be dead.

I will be dead, everyone reading this will be dead, everyone they know who is not a child will, in all likelihood, be dead.

Another 40 years on from there, every single one of the 7.8 billion people currently alive on this planet will be dead.

In fact, in the time it took you to read up until this point, 50 people just died. And by the time you reach the end of this article another 150 will have, as they say, 'passed over'.

If someone had the ability to demo an ultra high-speed time lapse of a 100 years of human society within a minute-long video, human beings would look like bubbles in a stream. Emerging out of thin air and popping in quick succession.

Within a 100 years from now barely a handful of people will have any memory of you. And by 2200 CE, it's quite likely no one will know you ever lived.

What this means is that your entire existence will seem like it never even happened.

Forget immortality, even your mortal existence will be nothing more than hearsay.

Before you assume that I'm saying all this to point to how utterly insignificant and inconsequential a human life is in the grand scheme of things… I'm not.

Quite the opposite.

Instead, I marvel at the fact that something so momentary and purely incidental, no more stable than a bubble, can experience something so seemingly profound as a life.

And not just a life, but some things as profound as love, fear, joy, doubt, friendship, curiosity, rage, forgiveness, passion, learning, understanding, hope, despair, grief, catharsis, realization.

A single speck of consciousness so fragile, gone before it barely even had a chance to settle. Yet, the depth of experience that is available to this speck is the entire history of our universe itself.

A single flicker of consciousness so fleeting, that most will never even have seen its flame. Yet, that flicker has light enough to reach across space and time.

A single pulse of sentience so brief, yet with the capacity to (in the words of William Blake's *Auguries of Innocence*):

Hold Infinity in the palm of your [its] hand
And Eternity in an hour

Others may forget your name.
It matters not. You know what it is.
Others may not even know of your existence.
What does it matter? You know that you are.
Let others call you a mortal.
That is what they see. Yet, you who cannot remember being born and will never know your own death are an immortal to yourself.
As brief as they say a lifetime is, to you it is all of eternity.
This is as short and sweet as it gets.

Chapter 24
PICK YOUR POISON

The basement smelled like beer and hockey equipment. Ten guys in various stages of intoxication roared, yelled and guffawed boisterously as cards were dealt across the felt table and clay chips fell like stacks of dominos. My opponent, a burly goalie, wearing shades and his varsity team's hat turned backwards, had me engaged in a death stare as he tried to get a read. The moment just before, I had said those two words that make any poker enthusiast's adrenaline pump:

'All in.'

I gazed back at him coolly, revealing nothing yet silently encouraging him to take the bait. After a long pause he responded, 'I call.' He revealed his pair of Kings which gave him the full boat: Kings over two's. The guys around him thumped him on his back and congratulated him on what looked like a sure win. That is, until I revealed the pair of measly deuces in my hand.

'Four of a kind,' I said.

The room erupted in mayhem as nine hockey jocks whooped and chest bumped and beer went spraying everywhere. The burly dude sat motionless uncomprehending. I gathered up the cash on the table and said, 'Thanks for the rent, ladies! Let's do this again sometime…'

I stepped out into the crisp summer night and began walking briskly back home. It was 1 am and I felt good about the four hundred dollars in my pocket. I thought about the warmth of my room, the last two chapters of *The Brothers Karamazov* I was eager to finish reading while listening to some Chopin.

I was only a few feet from my front door when my cell phone began vibrating.

It was a friend of my mother's saying something about his son being in trouble and that he needed my help. I didn't really understand but the urgency in his voice sounded genuine. He said he needed to meet me at a gas station 30 minutes away. So, I got into my car, still partially intoxicated, and drove.

Earlier that morning I'd just flown back to Toronto from California. The whole family, from different parts of the States and Canada, had gathered in San Francisco to celebrate my grandma's 75th birthday. The celebrations over, they had then planned a family trip to Yosemite. I wasn't able to join them, since I had a job interview in Toronto the next day.

Driving towards the gas station, I recalled my cousin taking me to the airport that morning. He was the closest thing I had to a brother. We had lived together through high school when I'd moved in with him, his older brother, my aunt and my grandma. They were my family, closer in many ways to me than my own parents.

After graduating high school, however, we saw each other infrequently. A fact that we both felt needed to be remedied. Saying goodbye to him at the airport that day we promised each other that the next time we saw one another would be a lot sooner.

I pulled into the gas station to see a single car parked with its headlights on. Two men waited silently outside, both of whom I recognized as family friends. I got out of the car and waved to greet them but their expressions communicated to me that something significant had happened.

They began approaching me unsure of how to begin and I responded, 'What happened?'

'It was a car crash, a head-on collision. A drunk driver came speeding around the bend on the wrong side of the road. Your aunt, your cousin and your grandma are dead. I'm so sorry.'

'My mother?'

'She is alive. She was in another vehicle.'

'My sister?'

'She was the fourth passenger in the car. She was badly injured and was air-lifted to the hospital. We don't know if she will make it.'

'I need a moment.'

I lit a cigarette and gazed up at the full moon. I planned out my logistics for the next few hours in my head. I had them drive me to my mom's place where I gathered a few clothes I kept there and a few things of hers and my sister's. Then I went to the airport and boarded a red eye to San Francisco. I kept the image of my sister in the forefront of my mind. I checked my heart to see how it felt. It felt calm. I knew she was still alive.

A few hours later I landed in SFO and was picked up by a family acquaintance I'd never met. First thing I asked, 'She's still alive?' And he answered that she was and that she was going to be taken in for surgery shortly.

'I need you to get me there before she goes in.'

We sped to the hospital and I made my way through the hallways towards the ICU. As I approached I saw the expressions of my mother, my uncle, other cousins and aunts, their faces devastated by grief at the carnage. I held my mother who was incoherently repeating their names over and over.

I entered the room where my sister lay still conscious. She smiled weakly when I walked in. I told her she looked like shit and that made her laugh and then wince in agony. They said the impact had been so intense that the rear seat-belt had sliced through her body. The lower belt had torn through her intestines and the diagonal belt had dissected her aorta just below her heart. All that held the two halves of the aorta together was a single string of flesh no more than a few millimeters wide. They didn't think she'd survive the night.

She survived the surgery on her stomach that day. But the aorta was another matter altogether. My uncle being a surgeon himself and well-connected in the field had contacted nearly every expert in the country about her case. No one was sure what to do. Any attempt to intervene would have been too risky. So, they decided to take a wait and watch approach. They gave her a generous 2% chance of survival.

Over the next two months my mother and I practically lived in the hospital. My mother prayed a lot during that time. She asked me why I didn't and I told her there was no reason to. I somehow knew this wasn't my sister's time.

There was another nineteen-year-old Latina girl in the ICU with a head injury from a car accident. Her family also waited with us every day outside the ICU. Every morning they'd stand in a circle and pray together. One morning they were informed that their daughter was still in a coma and it wasn't looking good. That morning I joined them in their prayer circle. I knew deep down she wasn't going to make it. Later that evening, she died. The waiting room emptied. Then it was just Mom and me for another month as others came and went.

Two months later my sister was transported by Lear jet to a hospital in Toronto. She was out of the woods. Her aorta had miraculously fused itself back together with scar tissue, something that her consulting surgeons still marvel at today. She spent another couple of months recovering before she returned home.

At the funeral of my aunt, my grandma and my cousin, I was unsure what it would feel like to see them lying there. I had been wracked with grief for the entire week since the accident. Yet, when I saw their lifeless corpses in their caskets a feeling of calm washed over me. It wasn't them. It was only their bodies. I felt it viscerally in that moment just how little of the essence of a being exists in their physical manifestation.

Morbidity and Mortality

I am not a huge advocate of meditation these days, although I once practiced intensely. However, there is a kind of meditation that I still continue to do quite often. I call it my morbidity and mortality meditation.

It's not a formal practice by any means. Just something I engage in when I am by myself: typically on long drives or sitting in a park somewhere. And what I do is I intentionally envision scenarios of great suffering both of myself and that of others.

For instance, I begin by envisioning the death of my loved ones. I envision the sudden death of my wife and the moment of finding out. And I allow my mind to vividly immerse itself in the story of everything that unfolds afterwards. The shock of finding out, communicating the news to her parents. Approaching our two little daughters and holding them through their disbelief and inability to fully process. Being a single widowed parent grieving in a home that feels vacant without her laughter, her voice, her scolding, her infectious energy. I go into this story and I live it fully for a long time.

On another day I may envision the death of my older daughter and the torment that transpires after that. Holding her lifeless body in my hands, unable to comprehend the fact that she isn't here with me. The grief that follows. How it destroys us. I then separately live out two scenarios. One in which my wife and I separate unable to reconcile the grief. Another where we somehow pull through and are stronger for it.

Then on another day, it's the loss of the younger one I imagine. Or the loss of both our children. Or that of my wife and the oldest. Or on another day, the loss of all three. In each case, it is not so much the event but the aftermath that is my focus, the living out of which causes a suffering that feels as real as if it were to really have happened.

But it isn't only death scenarios that I envision. It's also other forms of traumatic experiences. Our child being abducted and us having to live through the nightmare of constantly searching for her and never knowing what happened. Being in a crash where my entire body is paralyzed, and I am forced to eat food through a straw for the rest of my life. Or my wife being diagnosed with a degenerative disease like Alzheimer's and how our life is transformed by it. Or driving distractedly and accidentally killing a child, then spending the rest of my life in prison away from my own family.

The experience is so visceral sometimes it makes me sick to the point of wanting to vomit. The mixture of shock, misery, rage, revenge that courses through me is such a potent cocktail. Sometimes I have to bail in the middle because it's too much to bear.

Living out these lives in my mind is something I do because I know someone somewhere has lived it for real. Someone somewhere has suffered in that way, and until I can envision myself in that same place, they are forever separated from me.

Each time I emerge from one of these meditations, I feel emotionally fatigued yet brimming with joy and gratitude for the life I am living. To find my wife alive and well, my children laughing and mischievous, feels like raising them from the dead over and over. To find myself free and healthy gives me an appreciation for legs that can still walk, a mouth that can still chew and the fact that I can step out of my home and into the fresh air at will.

Small Doses

I saw a fascinating news story once about an unusual gentleman, named Steve Ludwin, who routinely injects himself with snake venom. He began doing it on a whim when he was only a teen. The first time he did it he injected an infinitesimal amount, hardly even a drop. The pain that he felt, he reported, was excruciating, unlike anything he'd ever felt before. He felt his veins would explode and his entire body felt as if it had been doused in kerosene and then set ablaze. After that he vowed he would never do it again… but his curiosity got the better of him.

Over the years, he began injecting himself with progressively larger amounts of venom because he began to notice that his general health, strength, stamina, energy levels, focus, memory and moods had begun improving. As he studied and experimented he developed an injection regimen of different venoms of varying potency.

Today, more than thirty years later, he is in his fifties yet looks significantly younger. And he is the subject of scientific experiments worldwide that test his skin, blood, organs, muscles, bones and DNA for anti-aging properties. These experiments claim that his body deteriorates at a much slower pace than other people's and his cells are able to regenerate remarkably fast.

I don't recommend anyone follows Steve Ludwin's example, goes home and shoots themselves up with snake venom by any means. But the intuition that led him to experiment in this manner is a phenomenal one.

What doesn't kill you only makes you stronger sounds like a cliché but in this case it is true. Unlike Steve, rather than snake venom, I inject myself with controlled doses of my own poison of choice… psychological suffering.

And I have found that when you inject a sound mind with a prescribed dosage of suffering the mind begins to adapt and develop a more robust response. Just like Steve's body was able to accept more potent doses over time, my mind is able to process suffering now in much higher doses than I could in the past. Its capacity for acceptance has grown greatly. And my psychological health is better for it. It feels energized in its outlook and is able to bounce back rapidly from disaster. It is able to function optimally in a crisis.

My capacity for empathy has increased a hundred-fold from what it was. And it wasn't 'love' that did it. It was small, consistent doses of suffering.

When I see people in spiritual circles going on and on about how compassionate they feel and engaging in compassion-expanding practices like *metta* (loving-kindness) meditation where they send love and well-wishes to those who are suffering, I can't help but shake my head.

I shake my head because you don't develop compassion by sending others love from the safety of your own comfort zone. That isn't how it works. You do it by immersing yourself in their chaos. And if you are able to emerge from that chaos with even a shred of self-understanding, then that is your act of compassion.

The only way to expand your heart is to bore into it and hollow it out. And within that feeling of utter chaos, hopelessness and void, lie the lessons of freedom.

Immersing yourself in that pit of despair with another and then clawing your way out may not show them the path they need to take. But it may give them the courage to know that it can be done.

Chapter 25

ONCE AGAIN MOUNTAINS

Q: I struggle to understand why you engage in that kind of meditation you talked about in the *Pick Your Poison* article. I spent so many years imagining all kinds of horror scenarios. It's caused me so much anxiety and depression. Taking drugs and binge eating were the only things that helped me cope. I was addicted to them. Finally, by reading Byron Katie and other teachers I came to see that I am not my thoughts. I am that which witnesses the thought. *I am awareness*. That was the turning point for me. Before that I was on a one-way street to hell. But understanding that I am awareness gave me space from my own mind. It allowed me to step out of the story of the little me. And there is no way I would ever go back to living like that.

Why would I want to go back to imagining these scenarios of pain and suffering in the same way that you do? That feels like taking a step backwards. But at the same time when you talk about it it doesn't sound like a step backwards. I feel in my intuition that it sounds like a step forwards. I'm just struggling to see how. Maybe you can help me see it?

A: That's actually a great question and I want to thank you for asking it. You're not the first person to ask it, but the way you've worded it here encapsulates all the concerns and objections others have had.

To begin, let me clarify that when I write my only purpose is to share my own outlook, my own experience and my own process. It is not intended to be some sort of instruction manual on how others should go about their own lives. What a person does with my words is entirely up to them. No one has to do it my way.

If others find some common points and resonance and find certain approaches that I have taken relevant and applicable to their own lives then that is their prerogative. And if some find absolutely no relevance that is also not really of much concern to me. I see, I think, I feel, I reflect, I express as feels natural and necessary to me. It may not be that way for someone else. For another it may feel utterly unnatural and unnecessary.

Some people tell me that what I say is nonsensical garbage. I've also heard people say that it is one of the most honest renditions of truth they have come upon. I personally have no desire to prove any of these people either wrong or right. All these things are their experiences of my writing, not mine. My experience is something different entirely.

What I would suggest to anyone reading my words is to keep an open mind with a healthy skepticism. You don't really know me. All you have is my words. For all you know I could be making all of this shit up. Trust your own intuition on the matter and follow through on that.

Having said that, let's address the question at hand.

I am not my thoughts.

This one statement is taken as a fundamental truth in many contemporary spiritual teachings. But as with everything that can be expressed in the form of language it is only a half-truth. The other half of that truth, of course, being, *I am my thoughts.*

Huh? one might say. What are you talking about?

I'm talking about mountains.

Now I don't want you to think I'm being facetious so allow me to clarify.

Like you, I spent the greater portion of my life traumatized by the thoughts in my head. Like you, I believed quite unconsciously that *I am my thoughts.* Therefore, everything my thoughts say to me must be true. They must contain a nugget of reality. I was willing to doubt certain thoughts I had about my environment, circumstances and other people, but what I seldom doubted were my thoughts about myself. Self-referential thoughts. Those somehow came to be taken as set in stone.

Like you, I spent inordinate amounts of time projecting various scenarios of doom and gloom. I would worry, fret, suffer tremendous anxiety and panic over such envisioned scenarios. I would constantly replay events in my mind, imagine doing things differently and then get down on myself for reacting the way I did. I would torture myself for hours fantasizing about the things that would probably never happen. Believing *I am my thoughts* was a lot of fun. So much fun that I regularly contemplated popping pills or slitting my wrists in the bathtub. (I always envied the jumpers. Never believed I had the courage to do it that way.)

So, you can imagine my great disappointment when my burning desire for a glorious send off was unceremoniously doused by this inconvenient little interruption called an awakening. For the first time I became aware of something beyond just a thought, just an emotion, just a sensation. I woke up to the visceral realization of being something else entirely.

Later, I found great validation in various spiritual books which allowed me to solidify this new perspective, this new point of view: *I am not my thoughts. I am that which is aware of the thoughts*. With the precision of a surgical knife, this singular shift of perspective sliced through my life, separating it into two discrete phases that felt so diametrically opposite that they may well have happened to two different people entirely.

The first phase incorporated this guy called Shiv who was miserable, self-loathing, arrogant yet inwardly insecure, highly social yet profoundly lonely and, most importantly, absolutely at odds with himself.

And then there was the second phase, incorporating *this new Shiv*: calm, inwardly free, self-loving, solitary, introverted and at peace with himself. In fact, this guy felt so unlike that other guy that I felt tempted to change his name to an Indian name along with the rest of those awakening types. Except, my name was already Indian so changing it to another Indian name would have been absurd. That's like Bob becoming Mike. It doesn't say transformation in quite the same way. For a while I tried writing under my Japanese nickname *Shi-bu* but that just became too pretentious after a while.

Yet, over time I began to feel an inner strain. I couldn't quite put my finger on it. There was a kind of stiffness in my being. And it took me a long time to figure out what it was.

As someone who works out with weights, I am familiar with the tendency that many muscular guys have of constantly being self-conscious of their bodies. They tend to hold their bodies in a stiff manner, often flexing muscles that have no need to be flexed or assuming postures that highlight their physiques. It all happens quite unconsciously. Quite often, it feels good to pose and flex in this manner. The body feels stronger when it is tensed than when it is in a relaxed state. What this also means is that gym rats are hyper-aware of their bodies all the time, far more than other people are.

I began to notice a very similar stance within my awareness. I found that I was hyper-aware of my thoughts at all times and preoccupied with not identifying with them. It's not that I would push them away. I'd let them come and express themselves. But I was always wary of them. My own thoughts had become these undesirable manifestations that I had to tolerate, and my mind was this inconvenient tenant squatting in the real estate of my consciousness.

Over time, I began to notice that my emotional responses to situations in life were becoming muted. The highs and lows began to fade and sort of flatline. Nothing excited me too much.

Nothing bothered me too much either. It was all sort of what it was. I, of course, took this as a sign of great progress. One step closer to that holy grail of equanimity every cheap Buddha statue in your house exudes. I believe the exact thought, *So this is what the Buddha must have felt like,* did saunter across my mind on occasion. Funnily enough, I didn't feel too inconvenienced by the thought.

Along with my own emotional numbness, my empathy began taking a nosedive as well. I simply couldn't identify with people who seemed to be suffering in the world. It wasn't that I was dismissive of them or attempted to minimize what they were going through. It's just that the explanation was quite simple: they were believing their thoughts and this is what believing your thoughts does. It causes suffering.

I couldn't see what a callous response that was at the time, no matter if there was some truth in that sentence. It would be like a doctor remarking to someone who is dying of lung cancer, *Well, that's what smoking does.*

Over time I became completely desensitized to the suffering of others, to my own emotions, to my own fears, but also my own passions. Everything sort of went gray. And I kept up the posing and convinced myself that this was enlightenment. No desire, no fear, no attachment, no self. Awareness itself but minus the mind stuff.

It took me a long time before I finally realized that I was standing in an arid desert. I had literally divorced myself from everything that I had declared *wasn't me*. I had become the no-self of Zen scripture. I had shed the suffering self. And it felt so fucking incomplete. It felt like a shallow existence. Full of essence but lacking substance. How could that be?

Shallow were those material folks lost in their minds. Shallow were those still sleeping unaware of their own true nature as awareness. How could I be the shallow one? And yet, the feeling was undeniable. It all felt shallow and superficial.

Suddenly, all those profound spiritual books I'd read, all those teachers I'd watched all seemed equally shallow. The *Tao Te Ching* read like the *National Enquirer*[27], the teachings of Ramana sounded like an episode of *Keeping up with the Kardashians*. It was all empty at the core, missing something crucial. A bunch of half-truths parading as the whole of it.

Then, out of nowhere, when my first daughter was born something strange happened. I suddenly began to become acutely aware of the weight of my own body and the ground under my feet. And the love I felt for her was something indescribable altogether. I felt grounded. And I discovered a reservoir of emotion that I really had become quite convinced had dried up in me. For the first time in a long time I felt passion, and that twin emotion, fear, stir up in me. After all that time, their return felt fortuitous.

I felt a beating messy heart again, not just some disembodied pristine awareness. And I began to realize that I had become completely alienated from my own humanity. Humanity had become the obstacle, the source of suffering, and I had subverted it in order to discover my spiritual essence. Yet, this inner divorce had manifested itself as an existential estrangement. I can only compare it with the awkwardness of two parents under the same roof who no longer love or talk to one another, while at the same time there was the child within me who felt the impact of their alienation.

And so began the return journey of coming full circle within myself. Having differentiated myself from my own mind, now it was time for the integration to happen. The human journey is an existential calculus[28] after all.

For a person suffering from the burden of their own mental ruminations the act of divorcing one's identity from

---

27. *The National Enquirer* is a tabloid newspaper, famous for the publication of scandal and gossip.
28. Calculus: the mathematical study of continuous change.

the thinking and emoting process altogether can be just as effective as a scalpel is at cutting out a cancerous tumour. In other words, the effect is immediate and remarkable. However, the scalpel is always a last resort in cancer treatment since inevitably something of essence is lost in the process when such a drastic measure is employed: a breast, a prostate, a limb, an organ.

The moment we declare our own thoughts as unreal (and for some, even emotions as unreal) we cloister ourselves into a very narrow band of experience and are forever preoccupied with disowning any conscious experience which doesn't fit our definition of reality, as *not me*.

But what is *me*? We assume there is such a thing as 'consciousness' that is separate from the 'contents of consciousness'.

I am not my thoughts, we say, *I am the awareness of the thought*. But have you ever had a thought that you weren't aware of? Or vice versa, have you ever been aware without there being something to be aware of?

Separating out awareness from phenomena is a method of bifurcating reality that we perform because we are desperate to somehow get ahead of the game. We don't want to feel like we are constantly being played. We want to feel like we have some control, some autonomy in all of this.

Yet, when I look into my own conscious experience the only version of *me* I can find is as a steady unbroken stream of conscious phenomena—thought, sensing, emotion, thought, sensing, sensing, emotion, thought, thought, sensing, ad infinitum. In other words there is no *I* that is separate from what I am aware of. In each moment as the phenomenon changes so does the shape that the *I* takes.

There is no thought without an *I* to think it, there is no emotion without an *I* to feel it and no sensation without an *I* to sense it. Similarly, the only form in which *I* have ever occurred is in the form of a thought, emotion or sensing.

Form as essence. Essence as form.

Inextricably interwoven. Indistinguishable. One can no more separate them than one can separate water from wetness or fire from warmth. Wetness is the essence of water. Warmth is the essence of fire. Without one another they are merely abstractions. They are nonsensical.

Awareness is the essence of thought, emotion, sensation. Thought, emotion, sensations are the forms of awareness. Without one another they are abstractions. Just as nonsensical.

There is a famous zen saying attributed to Seigen Ishin:

Before I had studied Zen for thirty years, I saw mountains as mountains, and waters as waters.

When I arrived at a more intimate knowledge, I came to the point where I saw that mountains are not mountains, and waters are not waters.

But now that I have got its very substance I am at rest. For it's just that I see mountains once again as mountains, and waters once again as waters.[29]

It captures, in metaphor, the very essence of what I have expressed above.

If I were to convey his sentiment in my own words it would be something like this:

Before, I was my thoughts, and I was my emotions.

When I arrived at a more intimate knowledge, I came to the point where I saw that I was not my thoughts, and I was not my emotions.

29. A translation by D.T. Suzuki (2010). *Essays in Zen Buddhism*, London, Souvenir Press.

> *But now that I have got its very substance I am at rest. For it's just that I see I am once again my thoughts, and I am once again my emotions.*

Do you see?

Chapter 26

PORNLIGHTENMENT NOW!

He sits atop the stage, his half-closed eyes scanning the room dreamily. The silence is deafening, broken only by a sigh that escapes the lips of one of the audience members. Hundreds of eyes are fixed upon him, unblinking. Every person seated in that room is erect and throbbing with anticipation for that first touch of wisdom. Like mousetraps delicately set, each one's mind is taut and ready to snap. And then, slowly, deliberately, a single syllable departs from his lips and sails over the room like a feather before gradually drifting downwards and settling gently, ever so gently, upon their ears.

Gasps, moans, sighs and purrs of pleasure erupt in the room communicating to him that he has hit the E-spot. For the rest of the afternoon he will continue his verbal foreplay as the audience shudders, mmm's, aha's and weeps with abandon, unable to bear another moment of being so utterly tantalized.

Welcome to Pornlightenement, where your floppy, flaccid self-identity is massaged, aroused, hardened and then masturbated until you ejaculate awareness all over yourself. But not just once. Over and over and over again...

When I was thirteen I was motivated by a desire to seek truth. Yet, that desire was only secondary to an even more powerful desire. And that was the desire to get laid.

Of course, the fact that I was living in South India in a conservative Brahmin society meant that realizing that desire was an absolute impossibility. It was the closest thing to a concentration camp for horny teens. So, what did we desperately repressed boys do to realize our inner non-virgins? We watched porn. A lot of porn.

I still remember my first porno. It was a videotape titled *Hidden Obsessions*. I stole money from my grandmother's bedroom in order to rent it. I even put on shades and a long coat in order to look older than I was when renting it from the local bootleg store.

It was a terrible recording, clearly a cam print. But none of this mattered. I watched the tape over and over until the film frayed. When I finally returned it months later, the guy at the store didn't want it back. So, I watched it a few hundred times again.

We had a little porn enthusiasts club where we exchanged videotapes that we had 'borrowed' from video stores. And the more we watched the more we yearned. Yearned desperately for the day when we would finally be the ones doing what we could only dream of.

Every once in a while, I'd encounter a former high school graduate who had moved on to college. They would regale me with tales of their sexual exploits and I would listen in rapt fascination like a child listening to a fairytale. These guys were gods. More than gods. They were the sexually liberated. The sexually enlightened. And when they spoke, our hearts were filled with yearning and our testicles ached with frustration.

Four years of watching copious amounts of porn and I felt I knew what this sex thing was all about. I was ready. It was meant to be. Any day now, the moment would strike and my sexual *satori* would unfold. Perhaps, it would happen in a barn. Or I would go in for a checkup at the clinic and some sexy nurse would find me irresistible. Or at the library perhaps? My body was primed and on high alert during every waking hour. Because if I'd learned anything from the movies, it was that this stuff happens when you least expect it!

When it finally did happen, I was in college, I was drunk, I fumbled through most of it and I can barely remember any of it. But I was liberated!

Fast forward a few years and I was now on a different trip. I had been successful in losing my sexual virginity but now I was aiming for the big kahuna. How to lose my spiritual virginity? From what I had heard sexual union was only a shadow compared to union with the divine.

So, I began the process again. I began watching the videos, reading the literature. I watched the biggest stars in the pornlightenment industry: from the classic stoic heroes like Ramana and Nisargadatta who used simple old school moves to arouse and titillate to newer emerging stars like Eckhart Tolle and Adyashanti whose babyface innocence and crooning aphorisms fondled my heart and plucked on its quivering strings like a harp. And each time I'd watch, listen or read these guys my mind would develop a rock-hard erection and every gentle stroke of insight made it throb even more. And I'd be taken to the edge until, no longer able to contain it, my awareness would explode and I'd be left spent and trembling with aftershocks of epiphany after epiphany, unable to read another single word.

For about five minutes.

And then, off to the races again.

What most people fail to realize is that the spiritual industry has about as much to do with spirituality as the adult film industry has to do with sex. Obviously sex is the format in pornography but the real purpose here is *entertainment*. Porn is not meant to be sex education. It is sex entertainment. Similarly, spiritual teachers are not teachers, they are performers. And their job is straightforward. It is to entertain. To entice. To enthrall. To make you blow your existential load.

Which is why when you compare pornography to the satsang circuit certain stark similarities arise. There are a few A-list stars who do all the fucking. While the rest flock from star to star masturbating themselves voyeuristically.

There are genres in pornlightenment just as there are in pornography. There are genres that employ elaborate narratives, costumes, storylines, role-play and rituals, and there are those that go minimalist gonzo and stick to just humping/imparting wisdom. There are genres that specialize in specific fetishes like anal sex/non-duality. And then there are those that focus on certain culture appeals like busty Asians/Zen Buddhists.

Both industries depend heavily on merchandising, seminars, trade shows and celebrity endorsements. No matter if you're a superfan of a particular performer and choose only to watch that one, or if you are a sampler and like to watch a wide variety, rest assured there is something to satisfy the appetite of every kind of customer. They want you coming back for more. It's what the whole industry thrives on.

Repeat customers.

Now, there may come a certain point where you suddenly realize that there is something sort of bizarre about all of this. That, if you are taking this seriously as anything more than entertainment, there is something very messed up with your head. Watching people fuck is fine but it sure isn't the same thing as fucking. And no matter how much you watch them, it doesn't get you any closer to getting laid.

Similarly, watching people talk about life, realization, enlightenment, the divine, oneness, transcendence and all is fine if you're bored and have nothing better to do. But if you actually convince yourself that listening to even a minute of it is going to get you there, you are sadly deluded.

Real-life self-realization looks nowhere as glamorous as it does in the staged version. In the same way real-life sex doesn't look much like the porno films (unless you are role-playing some idealized fantasy in your head). Perfect hair, perfect make-up, perfect pecs, perfect abs, a 13-inch mallet and mandatory enemas are hardly the conditions in which the average person will find themselves. To top it all off, while Fabio's erection seems to be the abiding kind, most of us will experience the non-abiding variety. *Because that's just shitty real life... get over it!*

Pornlightenment filled a void inside me. It aroused me in a way nothing else could. For a brief moment I could be brought out of my ordinary suffering self into something vast, magical and transcendent. And that orgasmic high became an addiction. The addiction became a form of self-soothing and stimulation. And, unbeknownst to me, the very self I was seeking was being objectified and prostituted back to me in the form of vacuous hope and meaningless rhetoric.

It's part of the reason why I started writing *Advaitaholics*. Spirituality as entertainment is fine, but if you are driven to partake in this industry by a sense of wanton craving for something real then you are an addict. Words and the experiences of others will do nothing to satiate that lust. They will do nothing to fill that void. All they can do is exacerbate it.

Everything one goes in search of is a distraction and a decoy from what is real and immanent.

Chapter 27

GATELESS GATE

Q: A teacher I follow defines awakening as: *A sudden awareness that you are whatever you feel, think and see*. What are your thoughts on this? How does this relate to your own experience?

A: I would say the essence of what he/she is pointing to is correct. It's the wording that I find a bit problematic: in my experience, when an awakening occurs, there is really no *you* left in the equation that is aware of being 'whatever is felt, thought and seen'. There is simply awareness *as* feeling, thinking and seeing. There is no subject being reconciled with object. No *you* to reconcile with a *whatever*.

I see this as a problem with many teachings in non-duality. There is an attempt at a reconciliation where none is necessary. An attempt to fuse subject and object together instead of doing away with both entirely.

Part of the problem is created by language itself, which requires the subject-object dichotomy linked by the verb that serves to unite the two in some kind of relationship. When I taught English grammar to people in Japan, this basic sentence structure is one of the first things my students learned.

In our subjective experience, the 'self' is the eternal subject and experiences that happen to, within and around it are its objects. But the moment awakening occurs, that reference point of the self, itself collapses. There is no longer a subject and therefore no awareness of objects in the traditional sense of how we view them. What remains is only awareness in the form of thought, emotion and sensation.

So, it's not a *you* that discovers 'whatever is perceived'. Rather it is a dissipation of both the you and the 'whatever is perceived' simultaneously. What emerges is the thing that exists in the first place: that thing is *awareness*, untethered at both ends of the process.

In the end, all there is, is process.

What we call *subject* and *object* are freeze-frame point-in-time entities which really have no independent existence outside of the process itself. The verb is the only thing in the sentence that is truly happening. Similarly, what we call *you* is just a single instance of a process, frozen in time, to which we mistakenly attribute an independent entity.

Now, although this kind of sudden non-dual perspective may dawn in an awakening experience, it is not sustainable. At a certain point, a person *must* revert to a self-centric reference point to be functional within society. And if you doubt the veracity of this statement try the following exercise:

Try This

Go out into the world and try speaking to people in sentences that contain only verbs. It won't get you very far. And if we can't even speak from that non-dualistic perspective, then actually living in society, day to day, from such a perspective is practically impossible.

Our brains will eventually—and naturally—revert to a self-centric, subject-object duality-based perspective because it makes sense to do so, purely from a survival and operational standpoint. Just like it makes sense to go out and get a meal when you are hungry. Yet, when people try and claim a non-dual perspective, briefly revealed in an awakening, as their modus operandi, then the 'awakened' perspective emerges. In my opinion this is an aberration.

This is the problem with neo-advaitic culture. It attempts

to reinvent the self as a 'non-dual and awakened self'. There is no such self. Self *is* the source from which duality emerges.

We have found people making grandiose claims, such as: *I am the universe* or *I am life* or *I am love* or, worst of all, *I am awareness*.

That's nonsense.

What they don't understand is that this duality of subject and object is like a seesaw that gets its balance on the fulcrum of the verb. *Self* and *world* exist balanced on the fulcrum of awareness.

The non-dual perspective is not the object and subject uniting to become one, like a seesaw folding back onto itself. It is not some new super-awakened self being born. It is the collapse of both arms of the seesaw simultaneously until the only thing left is the fulcrum. Awareness alone.

Thus, there simply is no such thing as an 'awakened self'. That's an oxymoron.

Either there is only awareness—this is the true non-dual perspective revealed in a *satori* experience. Or there is a type of subject-aware-of-object awareness, which is our everyday normal functioning awareness as a self.

There is no 'I-am-awareness' type awareness. Ever. That is a made-up story that gurus and teachers will sell you to try and co-opt their point-in-time awakening experience and sell it to you as their consistent normal daily functioning awareness. It simply is not true. It is bullshit.

And if you are still struggling to wrap your head around this, consider this analogy.

You can think of a *satori* as a great orgasm. Let's say there's a time and place where you've never had sex, but I have. Let's even say that I orgasm fairly frequently. That still doesn't mean that I live in a permanently orgasmic state. If I did, how could I ever function in society? Imagine someone enthusiastically, noisily and messily climaxing at a board meeting or a PTA meeting or while getting groceries at the store.

But if I can convince you that such a permanent orgasm is possible, especially to poor you who is still a virgin, then as long as I keep you massaging away and waiting for the glorious moment of climax, I can keep you captivated and listening to me.

That heightened awareness that many devotees claim in the presence of their guru is nothing more than an arousal response. It's no different than the sexual arousal one feels when watching a sexy woman or man. It is the charisma of the guru, coupled with an atmosphere pregnant with anticipation, which creates that sense of arousal in a follower and the heightened awareness.

However, if I simply told you the truth: *Hey listen! An awakening is just a temporary experience of blowing your existential load after which you go right back to being who you are and doing what you do*—well, that might sound somewhat interesting but it's unlikely to convert into a lifelong obsession for you.

In the end, all this hoopla about awakening is really a whole lot of hype. It's like a bunch of nerds in high school fantasizing about what it would be like to finally have sex. Waiting for that fateful day when they may finally enter that 'gateless gate'.

But the view from the other side is always one of: *Well, that was fun but no real biggie. Back to life, back to reality.* Certainly not worth writing home about.

That is, if one is being truthful, of course.

Chapter 28

THE SAME YOU

Whatever happens or whatever doesn't. Whatever works out in your favor or whatever breaks down. Whatever you end up winning or whatever you miss out on.

It's still the same you.

Whenever you're up or whenever you're down. Whenever it seems clear or whenever it's all a haze. Whenever you feel driven or whenever you are at a loose end.

It's still the same you.

However you succeed or however you fail. However you make things work or however you struggle to. However life appears to hold meaning or however it seems to hold none.

It's still the same you.

Wherever the destination or wherever the road. Wherever life seems to take you or wherever it doesn't. Wherever life flows effortlessly or wherever it gets stuck.

It's still the same you.

Whoever puts a smile on your face or whoever brings you down. Whoever thinks the world of you or whoever thinks you are scum. Whoever loves and cherishes you or whoever despises you and wishes the worst.

It's still the same you.

Whomever you place above yourself or whomever you place below. Whomever you admire and would fashion yourself after or whomever you abhor and would want to be nothing like. Whomever you value as being worthy of your love or whomever you value not.

It's still the same you.

Whichever path you take at the fork, whichever opportunity you miss. Whichever lens you use to look at the past whether with gratitude or regret, whichever lens you use to perceive the future, whether with hope or dread. Whichever thought consumes your mind, whichever emotion rifles through your body.

It's still the same you.

Why ever would you believe there is anything you need to justify, why ever would you think there is anything to prove? Why ever would you believe there is anyone to emulate, why ever would you think there is something left for you to find? Why ever would you believe you need to become 'more' in order to truly 'be', why ever would you think that what you are worth is not enough?

Have you ever been anyone but this very same you?

No matter the names you give yourself, no matter the identity changes. No matter the roles you play in your life, no matter the responsibilities you have or lack. No matter the myriad ways in which you suffer, no matter all the sophistications you use to escape it.

It's still the same you.

Yet, it is so obvious that it insults our intelligence for it to be so evident.

And so we invent the question: *'what' am I?*

And lo and behold we create a world of infinitely complex forms.

We invent the question: *'when' am I?*

And lo and behold we create a universe of time; with a past and future stretching on towards infinity and a present so minuscule as if it were meant to be completely ignored.

We invent the question: *'where' am I?*

And lo and behold we create a world separated by great distances: physical, intellectual and emotional.

We invent the question: *'how' have I come to be?*

And lo and behold we create a world of infinite cause and

effect, reasons and rationalizations, theories and superstitions, science and religion.

We invent the question: *'who' am I?*

And lo and behold we create layers and layers of identities and categories within which we box ourselves endlessly.

We invent the question: *for 'whom' do I exist?*

And we create the 'others' in our lives to whom we are forever struggling to reach and relate.

We invent the question: *'which' is my fate?*

And we create a world of good and bad, right and wrong, dark and light, suffering and liberation, samsara and nirvana that we are forever navigating as if standing on a tightrope.

We invent the question: *'why' do I exist?*

And we create a world of language, belief, logic and reason in the hopes that if we invent just enough symbols and pointers they will lead us to where we are seeking to arrive.

Yet, no matter how many hoops you try and jump through, no matter how many twists and turns your life takes. No matter how complex you try and make things, no matter how much you try and simplify. No matter how enlightened you want to believe you are, no matter how ignorant you feel. No matter how many knots the snake ties itself into in order to find its own tail—the snake is still the snake.

And you are still the same you.

Chapter 29
DARK NIGHT OF THE SOUL

The light from the streetlamps streamed in pools of pale yellow on the snow-covered side walk. The night was the coldest it had been all winter. A fine layer of ice encased everything: trees, railings, trash cans, hydrants and power lines. The crunch of my boots on the frosted sidewalk echoed through the silence of a city fast asleep.

3 a.m.

A gust of icy wind stopped me dead in my tracks. For a second, I considered doubling back. But it was seeing Jerry's cheerful face at the usual spot that kept me going.

'Don't you have somewhere else you've gotta be?' he greeted, cracking a toothless grin.

'Nope. Don't you?' I quipped back.

'I would. But my wheelchair's frozen solid...' he laughed, extending his arm for a fist pump.

I gave it a bit of a jiggle then wheeled him into the 24-hour convenience store right around the corner. The turbaned man behind the counter frowned as we came in but I put my hand up.

'He's going to be a paying customer tonight.'

He shrugged and went back to reading his magazine.

'Sandwich?' I asked.

'Just coffee...' responded Jerry.

'You know you've gotta eat...'

'Not much of a body left to feed, son...' he grinned.

Jerry was a war veteran who had had both his legs amputated after Vietnam. Having been failed by the American system and after falling in love with a Canadian woman, he'd made his way up to Canada nearly thirty years ago. Decades later, when his wife died, he got to drinking heavily and eventually ended up on the streets. Now, he was in his mid-sixties but looked closer to eighty.

I picked up a sandwich and coffee for Jerry and paid. Then, I slipped the cashier a ten.

'Just a couple of hours, until the sun comes out,' I said in Hindi. The man nodded and motioned to Jerry to park himself in the back of the store.

'You gonna head to the shelter in the morning?' I asked.

'Probably...' Jerry replied in his usual nonchalant manner.

'Jer...' I looked at him dead straight.

'Yeah, I know. I will,' he sighed.

'Get there before eight if you want breakfast...'

Jerry nodded. Then he fidgeted nervously and his eyes, dark and hollow, inquired:

'Hey, son. You got something else for me?'

I glanced at the empty bottle in the brown paper bag that he was clutching on the seat beside him and knew what he meant.

'Nah, Jer. But there's more where that came from.' I pointed to the coffee cup in his other hand.

He smiled and seemed to relax, 'Thanks kid.'

'Who else is crazy enough to be out on a night like this, right?' I laughed.

'Monique is,' he grinned.

Standing motionless in the streaming streetlight, wearing a thick fur coat and nine-inch stilettoes, she seemed like someone out of a graphic novel. Her legs, mostly bare, were purple-pink from the cold exposure. Yet, her body language communicated not an ounce of discomfort. Her shoulders seemed relaxed, rather than hunched. On a night that would make even the hardiest of people shiver, she seemed to have completely surrendered to the cold.

She turned her head and smiled as she watched me approach.

'I was willing to bet I'd see you out tonight,' she said.

'Yeah, well it's a bit cooler than usual that's for sure. How you holding up?'

'Montreal's a colder bitch,' she smiled.

Monique was the same age as I was. She'd been raised in Quebec in a well-respected family and her father was a judge. But being a black sheep and, having struggled to feel accepted, she'd left home at fifteen and had made her way to Toronto. She got into college but struggled to make ends meet. So she dropped out and became a sex worker so she could save up money to pay for the rest of her school.

'I saw Jerry roll by about an hour ago,' she added.

'Yeah, I know. I just parked his ass in the Rabba's before he fuses to that chair for good...' I grinned. 'Do I need to do the same for you? Who the hell is even coming on a night like this?'

'My regulars...' she replied. I looked both ways down the street and saw not a car in sight.

'Smoke?' I offered her my open pack. She smiled and accepted.

We talked mostly about sports, she being an avid Maple Leafs and Raptors fan. By the time we stubbed out our cigarettes, a white minivan pulled up to the curb and the passenger window came down revealing the nervous face of a balding, middle-aged man in a suit.

'Regular?' I asked.

She nodded. 'Thanks for the company, dude.'

'No worries. Stay safe, yeah?'

'Always,' she smiled and got into the passenger side. The man shifted nervously under my glare and seemed thankful to peel away. I'd never been a pimp, but I could certainly play the part if it meant protecting my friends.

I cut through the park and found a park bench that had completely iced over. I sat up on the backrest with my feet planted on the seat and remained for the next hour simply watching the world hibernate in darkness...

In my final year of university, this was my nightly ritual. I'd read or study in my room all night until the clock struck three. Then, I'd set off for a walk through the city to see what I could see. This was the city's other face, one that most people largely ignored or were oblivious to. This was the time when people whom many considered to be the so-called 'dregs of society', emerged from their concealed spaces to show themselves. The junkies, the pimps, the gangbangers, the dealers, the hookers, the bums. The deep night was when people's skeletons came out of their closets.

And I'd walk until dawn broke. I'd witness the city's transformation from depravity to respectability. From despair to hope. As shutters went up and markets began to open, the smell of fresh fruit and flowers would gradually take over the stench of alcohol and vomit. The aroma of freshly baked bread would overwhelm the odor of cheap perfume and cigarettes. Observing the world transition from night to day was a priceless kind of education.

Still, I loved the night more. Despite the seediness, the wretchedness, the danger of it all, it had a certain innocence about it. It was raw and uncensored, with no veneer of sophistication. What you saw was what you got. There was no dressing it up and pretending it was anything other than what it was. Crime, addiction, sex for sale, homelessness, intoxication, fetish: every darker instinct within a human being on abject display without apology, without shame. There was a freedom in being able to witness the world express itself in this regard. The daytime pretenses, social niceties and illusions of respectability we all indulged in felt insincere in comparison...

What motivates most people towards spirituality is the desire to transcend suffering. We are convinced that a way of life is possible in which our experiences will be wholly positive, that our interactions can be free from conflict, that the natural state in which our circumstances appear can be one of peace and harmony. Isn't that what most people want? Peace in the world? Peace of mind?

And so, we invent a spirituality of so-called 'love and light' in an effort to escape the shadows. We want our spirituality to be respectable, moral, ethical and admirable. We want our ashrams to smell like fresh flowers and fruit. We want our homes to waft with the aromas of freshly baked bread.

Wholesome, harmonious, connected living.

But it's all a veneer. Because beneath the white linen façade is an underbelly of forgotten pain, seething aggression, molten lust, morbid fear and wild desire. This is the space of darkness and shadow concealed within us that many are too terrified to even acknowledge. It is the soul's 'dark night'.

And a spirituality that is afraid or unwilling to venture into this space, is a sham spirituality.

Many of you are familiar with the phrase *The Dark Night of the Soul,* the title given to the famous poem by the Spanish mystic St. John of the Cross, and later used by Eckhart Tolle in his book *The Power of Now.* The phrase is representative of the narrative arc of the spiritual seeker who must traverse through the darkness of his/her own ignorance in order to finally emerge into the light. It is an archetypal story that holds a lot of appeal for those who are suffering because it provides them with the proverbial light at the end of the tunnel.

But, it is an oversimplification that is ultimately misleading. Because none of this is a linear process. Nor is it meant to be.

The dark night of the soul, the way I have come to see it, is not some phase of our journey, it is a part of our being. The dark night is *of* the soul. It is a part of its very nature.

Just as the earth spins on its own axis, with part of the planet exposed to the sun and part in darkness, so also do we exist at all times in both light and in shadow. By analogy, a city thrives not only on the respectable and acceptable enterprises of the daytime, but also the clandestine, nefarious dealings of the night. We can take the analogy further to our understanding of ourselves—we humans are the product of all our motivations, both conscious and ulterior.

While we may convince ourselves that it is, in fact, possible to bring all of it above board, to illuminate and purify all that is base and undesirable within us—that is a flawed narrative.

Those who struggle to understand and refuse to accept the inherent darkness that exists within themselves, have yet to truly embark on their spiritual search. There is a fundamental difference between exploring the wilderness of a forest and pruning trees in your garden. One may call either of them *being in nature* but they are not the same thing. What most people call *spirituality,* is like the latter parading as the former.

A philosophy of love and light seeks to tame that wilderness within us so that we may feel safe and secure in ourselves. It seeks to soothe our anxieties and provide certainties where none exist. And all of this becomes abundantly clear the very first time we venture into our own dark places.

Seeing this was a complete game changer for me. Up until that point, I was always searching for something to move me closer towards the light. I felt the darkness of my suffering gnawing at my heels, threatening to envelop me and I had spent a lifetime fleeing from it towards that pinpoint of hope at the end of my tunnel. I hoped for deliverance, salvation, nirvana: to emerge into a world of light and to leave that darkness behind for good.

Yet, when I finally ran out of steam and was forced to stop, I began to see, for the first time, that this wasn't a search I had been on all along, it was an escape.

When we search for anything, even a set of car keys, where do we look? Do we restrict our search only to the lofty spaces? The tops of dressers or tables? Or do we also look at the baser places, the dark nooks under the couch, the dusty spaces behind the bed where things often remain concealed?

Then, why was I running in a beeline?

It struck me that to know myself fully, I had to be willing to be exactly as I was and to explore it all, including all the darkness. And through venturing into the dark night of my own soul, over and over, I came to recognize some of the characters that resided there. The same Jerrys and Moniques, whom I had once encountered in the city and befriended, lived within me as well. The same malevolence and aggression that I had perceived in the eyes of some of the thugs and dealers I would pass, lived within me. The same desperation and vacant despair that filtered through the hollowed eyes of the crackheads I'd find strewn on the sidewalk, lived within me. The same cruelty and exploitativeness that some of the pimps exhibited, lived within me.

I began to see that my soul was an embodiment of every human desire, fear, hope, cruelty, triumph and suffering. That it was capable of anything and everything. And seeing it all within myself, I resisted the urge to recoil in disgust and instead allowed my natural curiosity to take over the exploration.

In this way, I stopped running altogether. As the fear subsided, what emerged was an acceptance of the human condition as a whole. And in that acceptance, I myself became whole.

Today, when I look out at the world and its events I understand and identify with everything that I see happening. I understand and identify with the progressive voices desperately attempting to bring a spiralling world into the light. I understand and identify with the voices of regression resisting in order to draw it back into darkness. Each one feeling misunderstood by the other. Each one feeling neglected by the other. Each one believing that to give in would be to succumb to chaos and the destruction of everything familiar, everything that is of worth.

I know because that is what I have lived through within myself.

Yet, there is no heroic emergence into permanent light. And there is no apocalyptic spiralling into permanent darkness. There is only constant movement from darkness to light to darkness to light.

A worldview that projects love as its ideal, ignores the hate that also naturally resides within. A worldview that projects knowledge as its ideal, ignores the ignorance that also naturally resides within. A worldview that projects peace as its ideal, ignores the aggression that also naturally resides within. A worldview that projects compassion as its ideal, ignores the cruelty that also naturally resides within.

And if you think you are incapable of hatred, ignorance, aggression and cruelty you do not know yourself.

All you have successfully done is orchestrate a life in which none of these aspects have had an opportunity to show themselves. And you may or may not have the opportunity to get acquainted with them in your lifetime. But if and when they eventually emerge, they will blindside you in a way you never knew possible and change the landscape of your life completely.

A spirituality of 'love and light' is really a spirituality driven by fear. Whereas a spirituality that willingly explores the dark underbelly of the soul is really a spirituality driven by love. That is the paradox.

Because only by accepting what we consider truly 'other' than us, do we discover that that other is also a part of us.

In this way the light of day and the darkness of night are brought together in one seamless full circle.

I only learned love, when I came to accept the hatred I am capable of.

I only began to understand, when I came to accept that I can never really know.

I only found peace, when I came to accept that I am fundamentally a dangerous creature.

Chapter 30

THE LAST HOUR

In the end, it's very simple.

You have only one more hour to live. The end is imminent. There is a meteor or an unprecedented natural disaster about to strike. There is no escape. The only choice remaining is what you are going to do with this last hour...

So, what do you do?

Do you reach for your meditation cushion? Do you sit with a teacher and listen to them pontificate about the illusory nature of self? Do you engage in a philosophical debate about the nature of existence? Do you intensify your search and seek to awaken even more intensely now that you've all but run out of time?

Or do you instead gather around with loved ones? Do you laugh, cry, hold one another and express gratitude for this opportunity you've had to share a story together? Do you go for a walk in nature in silence? Do you breathe in the air more fully, with appreciation for this fact of being alive? Do you brew a last cup of coffee or tea and sip it slowly? Do you read your child a story book? Do you kiss your partner and make love to them one last time?

The strange irony is that the meaning we spend a lifetime seeking becomes incredibly evident when there is no time left to seek it. When there is no future state to arrive at, no future point in time to project, everything becomes profoundly obvious and simplified.

This is as good as it gets. And what we see, what we have, what we are surrounded with suddenly begins to brim with meaning and essence.

And all those things that once preoccupied our attention—the seeking, the yearning, the endless philosophical conversations and debates, the practices, the books, the talks, the retreats—suddenly begin to pale in comparison. All our striving and our seeming achievement appears perfectly hollow when faced with the significance of what the final hour of being alive has to offer.

In that final hour, the whistle of the kettle piercing through the silence sounds more profound than the wisest words ever spoken. Your partner's smile brings a greater ecstasy than the greatest insight or revelation. Taking a deep breath is more fulfilling than any imagined state of peace you could ever hope to achieve. Feeling the ground beneath your feet is infinitely more reassuring than the promise of enlightenment.

Yet, in our everyday lives, we live as if this isn't the case. The final hour is something that only exists in our imaginations. Death is an abstraction at best. Something that happens to other people. And so, by robbing ourselves of the reality of death we rob ourselves of what is meaningful. We take for granted the very things that are of essence and instead seek that essence in places it doesn't exist.

We fail to see that the fulfillment we have been seeking all along is already inherent in the very fact of our being alive. That the enlightenment we have been seeking all our lives is already inherent in the very fact of our being aware.

Chapter 31

BASELINE HAPPINESS

Someone recently asked me if I consider myself as being happy.

And I responded that I do. He said that he considers himself happy as well.

I asked him what his criteria for happiness are and how he has established this happy state of affairs for himself. He responded that he endeavors to elevate his consciousness and conscious experience at all times.

I asked him what he meant by that, if he could provide me with a few examples, and he was glad to oblige me.

He said that in his day to day, he attempts to see the best in any given situation. He attempts to maximize his opportunities. When he meets people, even strangers, he attempts to connect with them from a place of pure being. He attempts to see the being in them as a reflection of his own essence and he feels a genuine love for them as a result of doing this.

I asked him if he feels like this consistently. And he responded that some days it is more natural than others. Some days requires greater effort because the mindset of separation keeps dragging him back into his 'old conditioning'.

He said he meditates twice a day in order to reconnect with the spaciousness and each time he finds his mind slipping back into habitual thinking he takes a few moments to sit and return to that space of stillness. He makes it a point to practice gratitude for all the things he has, for the people he meets, for nature. He stops on his walks often and gives thanks to the trees and the birds. This fills him with a sense of well-being.

When with family or friends, he tries not to get sucked into the drama in which they get lost. He can clearly see people's 'pain-bodies' and even see how his own pain-body is easily activated by them. And so he remains vigilant so as not to get drawn into conflict and thus maintains a peace of mind, even in the midst of it all.

When he is alone, he is always aware of his own mind and thoughts. He is careful not to allow his mind to wander too much into negative thinking cycles. Each time he finds his thoughts deviating from the present circumstance, he gently draws his attention back to where he is at in the moment. And thus he is able to remain present, calm and happy.

So, I remarked that that sounded great. And that he had achieved what many people struggle to. He was pleased to hear me say that. And asked me if I wanted to share my own 'secret to happiness' with him.

I laughed and said that my secret was that I do exactly the opposite. He smiled in bewilderment and then asked me to tell him more.

So, I said that I don't try and see the best in situations. Sometimes what I see is good, sometimes what I see is downright rotten. I know a lot of it is my own projection and may not be accurately reflective of the situation itself, but I'm okay with that. My perspective will naturally improve as my vision improves and that has been on an upward trajectory for years now, so I have little to worry about.

When I meet people, I don't attempt to connect with them. I only connect if I feel an inspiration to, and then that connection happens by itself without my wanting or not wanting. It's always a special experience when that happens, but what makes it extra special is that it happens when I'm not expecting it.

Other than that, to me a stranger is just a stranger, a cashier is just a cashier. Of course, I know there is so much more to them, but for my own purposes as I move through the world that is all I need them to be. Every once in a while, the circumstances will suddenly require a stranger to reveal more of themselves to me, or for me to suddenly strike an unexpected connection with a cashier over something as random as a shared milk allergy. And when that happens I am always grateful for the fortuitous turn of events. But I don't seek such experiences.

I almost never meditate anymore. I have no draw to connect with that sense of spaciousness or silence. For many years I would sit in meditation for that express purpose. Now, that spaciousness seeks me out when I least expect it. I may be standing in line at the supermarket and, in the midst of a crowd and fluorescent lights, the whole room empties out and I'm standing in vast space. I enjoy that experience thoroughly, but then it's back to being in line among impatient grumbling customers and I'm fine with that too. Those moments of unexpected spaciousness feel like your favorite song suddenly coming on the radio. There is a certain joy that brings which isn't quite present when you intentionally play that same song off a CD.

When with family and friends I often get sucked into drama, gossip, conflict, shenanigans and whatnot. In the midst of drama I am well aware of the pain conditioning ('pain-body' as he called it) in others as well as myself coming up but I don't impede it from doing its thing. The way I see it, the pain has to resolve itself, I am not equipped to resolve it. And it will resolve itself by seeking scenarios that provoke it and bring it up to the surface to be witnessed again and again. My only job is to be present to witness it when it does. Not to tamper with it in any way.

When I am by myself, my mind wanders freely, like a wild animal, wherever it desires to roam. Whether laying down to rest in silence, exploring some dark alley of my psyche, gnawing restlessly on a single bone of thought over and over, simply daydreaming, strategizing about things that will become inconsequential in the next moment, complaining about something, somewhere, someone or simply humoring itself with nonsensical existential paradoxes (some of which have made their way into this book)—my mind is its own animal, a beast that does not do well when caged. In fact, our relationship of trust has been built over decades after I showed an initial willingness to set it free. It has since always returned without fail and has never let me down.

It is the direwolf to my Jon Snow.[30]

And so I told him that, although I am far from being a peaceful and calm person, I am happy nonetheless. In fact, happiness is pretty much my standard modus operandi.

On hearing what I have written above, my friend seemed a bit perturbed. He then asked me what I thought was the basic difference between his happiness and mine.

I remarked that his happiness seemed to require constant maintenance whereas mine pretty much maintained itself.

Then unexpectedly, his face began to quiver, and tears began streaming down his face.

I put an arm around him and asked him what he was feeling.

And he confessed that he was absolutely exhausted. The constant vigilance that he had been maintaining for all these years against his own mind had practically wiped him out. His happiness, he explained, was always driven by a deeper sense of anxiety. His peace and serenity were always contingent on whether he was able to cope with the darkness and frustration always lurking just beneath the surface waiting to swallow him whole.

The direwolf example I'd given him had been especially striking. He didn't have the same relationship with his own mind. His mind was something he couldn't trust and so he was always attempting to tame it, guide it, domesticate it, teach it a way of being that it didn't gravitate towards naturally. And he felt cruel as a result of it.

I told him that I understood. Because that's also how I'd

30. https://gameofthrones.fandom.com/wiki/Ghost

operated for many years.

'Then what changed?' he asked me.

I replied that I realized there are two kinds of happiness: one is a peak experience and the other is a baseline experience. And I'd gotten really good at hitting the peaks, but my baseline, whenever I did come down to it, was unacceptable to me.

Yet, the reality was that the peaks were short-lived and reached only by effort, whereas the baseline is where I naturally returned to when I was at rest. So, I asked myself: *Which one is more reliable? Should I focus on elevating my highest self or should I instead focus on the lowest version of me?*

And so I shifted my perspective. And I found that the lowest version of me was the lowest for a reason. There was no perfecting it, or elevating it. Who I got to be on my absolutely worst day, was a person I needed to accept. He was a horrendous little shit of a human and being him is what I'd avoided pretty much every waking hour using meditation, positive thinking and so on.

That version of me was far from happy. He was a miserable sod, unloved by everyone including myself. Alienated, misunderstood and alone—no wonder he was so damn unhappy. Stewing in his own misery and darkness for decades like a Gollum, his concerns were purely for himself, purely survival driven.

The moment I understood this, then the whole equation of happiness for me changed. Peak experiences became meaningless to me. I didn't care how many moments of pure joy I could successfully string together. If there were still aspects of me living in darkness and alienation, then happiness was not the case.

It's like when I look at India, the country where I was born. There is all this hype about economic progress and the wealth being generated there. Then I look at how that same wealth is distributed and the disparity is appalling. While the top 1% easily fall within the richest in the world the bottom 50% easily fall within the poorest of the world. That is not a sign of a prosperous nation. A prosperous nation is one in which the bar on the lowest income demographics itself has been raised to a standard of living that meets all our human needs of adequate food, shelter, clothing, health care, sanitation and safety. Scandinavian countries come to mind as an example.

So, the moment I began thinking of myself as less of a person and more of an ecosystem, the glaring imbalances became unavoidable. The word 'happiness' took on a new meaning then. A happy ecosystem is a balanced ecosystem.

Whereas previously my understanding of happiness was limited to feel-good experiences, this new understanding could accept that all kinds of experiences had their place. A balanced ecosystem still manifests aggression and violence. The wolf still hunts the deer. Bacteria and viruses still annihilate entire herds, flocks and groups. But it all happens in proportion, so that the ecosystem itself remains stable. Thus, there is an intelligence that transcends our ideas of good and bad experiences and is able to create that sort of an exquisite order.

So, also within myself, there were several competing and conflicting elements that nevertheless had the potential to manifest an exquisite order and experience of harmony if only it were guided by an intelligence beyond the one that my binary rational brain, which thought in terms of black or white, was capable of.

I learned to let it all be.

I learned to view myself through the eyes of a wildlife filmmaker. Observing, curious, fascinated, learning but never intervening in the dynamics as they were manifesting. Allowing it all to play itself out, the good parts and the shit.

And over time, the ecosystem did regain its balance as I had thought it would. And the end result was an overarching sense of well-being, harmony and happiness without needing to expend a single ounce of effort to achieve it.

He sat looking at me silently and smiled. I asked him why he was smiling. And he responded:

'It's like I've been waiting my whole life for someone to tell me what you just said.'

Chapter 32

SPIRITUALLY INCORRECT

Q: How do you think personality relates to 'enlightenment' (btw I know you don't like that word)? This one confuses me. A lot of these teachers project peaceful and kind personalities. You on the other hand can be a real a**hole! (No disrespect!) Lol!

A: First of all, how dare you call me a teacher!

Jokes aside, no disrespect taken because it is true. I can be an asshole (this is a sentiment attested to by my infinitely patient wife, friends and family). But of course, there are plenty of times when I'm the opposite. In fact, if I had to hazard a guess I'd venture that I'm channeling assholery about 10% of the time.

Your query is about personality and enlightenment. I reiterate that we are looking at a continuous process of ever-increasing clarity about self and reality, a process that every sentient being is undergoing and, whether one is aware of it or not, they are somewhat related—but only loosely. Contrary to what a lot of people believe (either overtly or subconsciously) gaining clarity doesn't radically alter one's personality. At least, that hasn't been my experience of it. In fact, if anything it allows the inherent personality to really shine through in a more authentic way.

Some personalities are naturally more expressive, some are more laidback. Some personalities are more aggressive and some more passive. Some personalities are more abrasive and some are warm, fuzzy and likeable.

A lot of so called 'teachers' are posers. They're putting on a front because that's what contemporary or indigenous culture and the students require of them. The sheer number of heart icons and saccharine compliments that fly every which way in the online presence of this culture is quite gagworthy. But that is what has happened to spirituality. Spiritual correctness, not honesty, is what keeps much of the culture thriving. It really is no different than politics and society where the people who say all the right and sensitive words are seen as bastions of moral integrity, whereas others who may be a bit more open in their manner of speech are perceived as being moral Neanderthals.

The fact of the matter is, when a person has something at stake, then they will manipulate everything in their situation, including their own personality, in order to maximize the chances of a favorable outcome. It's why politicians smile so much and kiss babies. It's why spiritual teachers gaze understandingly and adopt soothing tones and extended pauses in their speech. They are tailoring their expression in order to induce a certain outcome—that outcome being people admiring or revering them for their wisdom, following them, talking about them, paying money for their merchandise and so on. Really no different than any other PR-type profession out there.

That's not enlightenment. That's show-business. That's not their personality, it's their game face.

None of this takes anything away from the influence some of these individuals have had, nor the wisdom they have shared. There is no denying that some are very insightful—but they are not honest.

In spirituality, as in politics, people are constantly watching the outward presentation, the body language and the behavior of the teacher. More than profound words, people want to sense a congruence between that person's insight and that person's behavior. This is a sort of naïveté on the seeker's part because the teacher is a human being, after all, equipped with the same personality traits, emotional experiences and frustrations as many of us. Yet, this unrealistic expectation that once they have realized something of the nature of reality, they must exude that kind of perfection in their temperament, personality, behavior and choices, is what creates a sorry state of affairs.

It all boils down to a very binary way of seeing life and human expression. We generally tend to think of expressions such as anger, doubt, fear, sadness, arrogance and frustration as being negative and thereby unenlightened. These, we believe, obscure our clarity of perspective. On the other hand, we perceive kindness, confidence, love, bliss, humility and calm as positive and thereby enlightened. We believe these enhance our clarity.

Yet, joy can obscure just as much as sadness. Love can distort just as much as fear. Excitement can obliviate just as much as anger. In truth, there are no such things as positive or negative emotional expressions. However, there is such a thing as balanced and imbalanced ones.

Psychological homeostasis is what occurs when one's expression is allowed to manifest organically. If one feels frustrated, then that frustration gets expressed or channeled in some way and it dissipates. If one feels joy, that joy is experienced or communicated and then it equally dissipates. However, the moment these expressions are interfered with, resisted, wallowed in or manipulated in any way—homeostasis is no longer the case. Now we have an ecological imbalance in the system.

Frustration resisted and ignored turns into seething anger, then rage, and eventually, when left to brew long enough, into violent outbursts. Joy when held onto and milked for too long turns into delirium and eventually mania. Doubt when indulged in turns into paranoia and eventually hatred. Peace when clung to turns into passiveness and eventually deteriorates into apathy.

Homeostasis is the state in which the human being experiences and manifests a natural balance. The experience of inner balance is the feeling of being grounded in oneself. And the manifestation of such a balance comes in the form of honesty—in thought, speech and action.

When the Buddha spoke about right thought, right speech and so on (the Eightfold Path) he didn't mean being 'correct'. Correct is an externally established consensus perspective on acceptable thought, speech and behavior. By 'right' he was pointing to the state of homeostasis within the organism: the right conditions within which everything exists in fine balance. And from these right conditions emerges right thinking, right speech and right action.

What those right conditions look like for each individual will differ entirely. Only the individual themselves can know for certain if they feel that sense of psychological homeostasis. There are no absolute external markers for it. What looks like peace on the surface could really be intense turmoil on the inside—expertly masked. What looks disorderly and haphazard on the surface could really be a wild and exquisite order on the inside.

A human being is after all a natural creation. And in nature, asymmetry is as much a manifestation of beauty as is symmetry. Ruggedness is as much a symptom of harmony as is serenity. And chaos as much a manifestation of perfection as order.

Clarity orients an individual to become first aware of, then prompted by, and eventually guided by homeostasis. The personality remains intact. Yet, that individual becomes organically oriented towards a right thought, speech and action rather than the correct one. And in doing so the individual experiences and expresses authenticity by default.

Chapter 33
NON-DUALUSIONS

What we call 'non-duality' seems to have become nothing more than a psychological strategy for spiritual bypassing, using the absolute as our rationalization tool for why things happen that we don't really understand.

What we call non-duality has become nothing more than a method of avoiding taking responsibility, for the choices that we make and the repercussions that those choices have, by claiming, *It's all inevitable anyway, so was there really a choice?*

What we call non-duality has become nothing more than a tool that we use to quickly resolve the cognitive dissonance that the apparently paradoxical nature of life produces within us because we abhor the uncomfortable tension that accompanies it.

What we call non-duality has become nothing more than a tactic for selectively rationalizing away our own flaws while actively highlighting the same flaws in others.

What we call non-duality has become nothing more than the misguided claim that because an absolute reality exists, the relative reality that we inhabit is an illusion and thus of little consequence; our endeavors, our enterprises, our relationships, our struggles, our triumphs, our fears, our joys are of little consequence since they are all formulated on the axis of a 'separate self' which has no reality.

Yet, the fact of the matter is that non-duality in its original form[31] says absolutely *none* of these things.

Non-duality simply states that the fundamental nature of

31. Advaita Vedanta.

reality is whole and indivisible. Every other conclusion we can extrapolate from that is just a distraction from the point.

So, let's look at some of the conclusions we have drawn from this basic statement of non-duality.

***

> **Conclusion #1:** 'Since reality is whole and indivisible in nature, the self is an illusion because it appears to be separate from the whole.'

This is a common fallacy among non-dual practitioners. This is why everyone is in an all-fire hurry to negate their self and claim that 'I am not here', 'there is no doer', 'no one is saying these words right now' and other absolutely absurd things.

Imagine reaching with your hand into the ocean and scooping out a handful of water and holding it in your cupped palm. You have separated the water from the ocean. To claim that the water is not separate from the ocean is a ridiculous statement to make. It is clearly separate. However, is the water in your hand any less 'water' than the water in the 'ocean'? Is it any more or less 'wet'? No, it is identical. In fact, 'ocean' and 'hand' simply refer to the shapes in which that water appears. Yet, its nature remains unchanged by the separation into the two containers.

So, there is a separation in form but not in essence. Yet, one cannot deny the separation in form and call it an 'illusion'. The nature of form is that it is created, it exists for a while, then dissolves back into the flux from which forms arise. Denying a form which clearly exists is ridiculous. That's like sitting on a chair and claiming that there is no chair. Until that chair breaks and disintegrates into dust, the chair is very much there.

Similarly, with the self.

As long as there is a body and a brain, awareness is organized into the shape of a self. That is the form in which it exists. Now, one might look at the universe and say, *The universe and I are of the same nature and* in essence *there is no separation between the two.* That is correct. Yet, many then continue on to say, *and because there is no separation, this self is an illusion.*

It is not.

That is like scooping water in your hand and claiming there is no water in my hand, when there clearly is.

Reality is whole and indivisible in essence, yet infinitely divisible in form. And this is the paradoxical nature of it. Those who are uncomfortable with paradoxes will try and assert one point of view over the other. And in doing so, they end up missing the whole point.

Form is emptiness, emptiness is form. [32]

***

Conclusion #2: 'Everything is inevitable, so there is really no choice to be made.'

This is a statement that is often used as a tool to encourage people to relinquish the iron-grip of control that they have over their lives. And from that perspective it has benefits. But when adhered to as gospel it has a totally debilitating effect on a person.

I had a friend who was terrified of driving. Each time she'd get into her car her seat would be completely upright and all the way to the front, with her nose almost at the steering wheel. And when she drove she gripped the steering so tightly her knuckles would be white. As a result, she was alarmingly hesitant in her driving and constantly second-guessed herself. The effect of this was that she was a hazard to other drivers because her reactions were unpredictable.

---

32. Taken from one of many translations of 'The Heart Sutra' or *Prajna Paramita,* readily available online.

So, I counselled her to relax. That there were things that she couldn't control. Her belief that if she stayed in absolute control she could ensure that nothing bad happened was a fallacy.

This helped her relax a little, and as she did, her driving became more confident.

However, imagine if she were to say to herself, *Well, control is an illusion and everything is inevitable so there is no point in me even holding the steering wheel.* That's a guaranteed car crash waiting to happen.

If you wouldn't relinquish your hold on the steering wheel of your car each time you get set to drive, why are you so determined to relinquish your hold on the steering wheel when it comes to your life?

I think part of the draw of non-duality is that it offers a respite from a culture of obsessive control. The current ideal of taking life by the horns and being masters of our destiny has infiltrated so deeply into our culture and psyche that it has turned us into neurotic creatures constantly seeking to control each and every little detail of our lives. Consumerism has inundated us with so much artificial choice in the forms of products and services that are marketed as 'essentials', that we are being faced with having to make 'critical' decisions thousands of times a day.

Take a person who is drowning in that sort of culture and tell them, *You know, it's all an illusion. There is no real choice in any of this.* And it feels like a hand literally reaching down and yanking them out of the water. It is no wonder that they then swing to the other extreme of attempting to relinquish all and any control over their own lives. It is the fear of drowning again that prevents them from being willing to even get their feet wet.

Claiming that 'none of this is in my hands' stops no one from gripping the steering wheel once the car gets moving. And if it did, they most likely never lived to talk about it.

***

> **Conclusion #3**: 'Time is an illusion, thus cause-and-effect are an illusion. So, since no one can know why things happen, it's best to reserve judgment about what happens.'

This is a famous strategy that many non-dual practitioners use to avoid dealing with the shit side of life. No one wants to be seen as being judgmental—as if showing judgment is somehow a *bad* thing.

No, judgment is crucial. It's what stops you from eating a rotten apple and picking a fresh one instead. Asserting one's judgment and saying, *This is a rotten apple,* isn't being 'judgy'. It is demonstrating common sense.

However, there is good judgment and poor judgment and good judgment develops with experience and the wisdom that emerges as a result of that experience.

Part of the the Serenity Prayer[33] most often quoted goes:

> *God, grant me the serenity to accept the things I cannot change, the courage to change the things I can, and the wisdom to know the difference.*

Wisdom lies in 'knowing the difference' i.e. good judgment. The cynic is one who sees rotten apples even among the fresh. The fool is one who claims that there are no rotten apples. Both show poor judgment.

Non-dual culture, in its reaction to the extreme cynicism of the world, has swung to the other extreme of encouraging a foolhardiness in people by relinquishing their basic common

33. *The Serenity Prayer,* as used in traditional 12-Step programs, is the first part of a prayer written by the American theologian Reinhold Niebuhr (1892–1971). *The Essential Reinhold Niebuhr* (1986). Yale University.

sense. Rather than encouraging people to show 'good judgment'. Instead, these admonitions encourage a person to show none at all. And the effect of that is that followers of this philosophy turn into something like adult infants: helpless, indecisive, taking no accountability, hoping to be cared for by their guru, their community, life or whatever.

***

> **Conclusion #4**: 'Everything that happens, good or bad, is simply part of *What Is*. So, there is nothing that needs to be done about it.'

Hitler was an animal rights activist, a vegetarian and an environmentalist who established many of Germany's progressive conservation laws.

Gandhi was a controlling husband, a negligent father and often slept naked in the same bed as his nieces in order to 'test his own self-control'.

Mother Teresa remained a vocal anti-abortionist till the very end and claimed that women who chose that path would go to hell.

Stalin was a doting father who always took the time to play with, educate and read stories to his children.

Paradoxes are uncomfortable because they require us to hold polar opposites in the palm of our hand. It is much easier to simply think of Hitler as demonic and Gandhi as heroic, Mother Teresa as saintly and Stalin as a monster. Yet, in reality even demons can be compassionate, even heroes can be perverse, even saints can be heartless and even monsters can show love.

But that's simply too complicated to bear. We want it simplified. We want good guys and bad guys. We want people we can love and people we can hate.

This is how the general public responds to the paradoxical

nature of life. By reducing it into a binary, black-and-white format.

The non-dual practitioner's response to paradox is something different altogether. Taking a black or white stance would immediately subvert their assertion of non-duality. So, they escape the paradox by claiming that it is all simply a manifestation of *What Is*.

Now, on the surface, this looks like a kind of acceptance, whereas in reality it is a subtle tactic of avoidance. We are uncomfortable with the paradox, we don't want to take a polarized stance on it, so we just sweep it under the rug of *What Is* so that we don't have to actually face it.

This attitude of avoidance breeds a culture of disengagement from our surroundings and what is happening within them. We begin to progressively cloister ourselves into our communities, our communes and our bubbles, all of which act as echo chambers of denial. And through this distancing, we gradually become desensitized to the suffering of other people, losing the empathy that is a natural aspect of what it means to be human.

To truly accept paradox means to engage with it. To be willing to *condemn* an action without condemning the person. To be willing to *commend* an action without commending the person. To fully face events and use our judgment to deal with them, without reducing their complexity in the hope of simplifying life. Never to avoid life events for fear of being hurt or blamed for showing poor judgment.

Simplicity is not simplification.

***

Conclusion #5: 'There is nothing to achieve, there is nothing to realize, there is nothing to actualize.'

This is another statement used by many to rationalize away their feelings of disappointment, confusion, guilt and sense of feeling lost. While the rest of the world is off pursuing this or that in the belief that achieving those things will enhance them in some way, seekers on the non-dual path swing to the opposite extreme. By asserting that one cannot be 'enhanced' in any way since one is already complete, there is no necessity to achieve, realize or actualize anything.

Again, this is a misguided conclusion to reach. We have no choice but to achieve, realize and actualize things as we move from one moment to the next.

When we are hungry we 'realize' we need to eat, we set out to 'achieve' that meal, we 'actualize' the meal by preparing and eating it. We then 'realize' we are satiated, we set out to 'achieve' some rest, we 'actualize' the goal by taking a nap and allowing the meal to digest.

Now, if on the other hand we are actively trying to *oppose* that process, then when we are hungry we *still* 'realize' it, yet we set out to ignore that hunger and thus 'achieve' a state of starvation. We 'actualize' our denial by manifesting an emaciated and weakened form. This is essentially the dynamic in anorexia.

So, the question is not whether it is necessary to realize and actualize. There is no way to short-circuit that process. Realizing and actualizing is happening anyway whether we want it to or not. The question is *what* we realize and *how* we actualize it.

If you engage with an open heart in the suffering of others you will actualize empathy. If you turn away in denial you will actualize apathy. There is no third option.

'Realizing' things with greater clarity will lead to the 'actualization' of realities that are more balanced and authentically aligned with who we are. One may argue, well what does it really matter? But that is a bullshit argument.

There isn't a person alive who isn't glad that they 'realized' that one shouldn't mess with fire. And the proof is in the fact that they haven't 'achieved' third degree burns all over their body. Instead, they have 'actualized' a healthy, intact form.

***

Non-duality, as a philosophy, seeks to examine the nature of reality, not to prescribe how human beings must live. That is something each of us must determine for ourselves on our own; by fully facing our circumstances, by learning to bear the tension that paradoxes present—rather than resorting to polar perspectives or washing our hands of them altogether. Denying the existence of our own separation and manifestation as an individual form, even if we are united in our essence, is the ultimate cop-out.

The attitude I have learned to take in my own life, is succinctly captured in this quote by Robert E. Howard, author of the Conan stories:

> *Let teachers and priests and philosophers brood over questions of reality and illusion. I know this: if life is an illusion, then I am no less an illusion, and being thus, the illusion is real to me. I live, I burn with life, I love, I slay, and I am content.*

Chapter 34

THE MYTH OF BEING AWAKE

The question on the mind of almost every seeker is, *How do I wake up?* But this is a meaningless question based on a myth. And that myth is that there is something called *being awake.*

At what point did you become an adult? Is there such a thing? We have, for the sake of convenience, created these clear-cut stages in a person's life. You're an adult at 21. But are you? I know 15-year-olds who are more mature than some 50-year-olds. Of course, the 50-year-olds have adult bodies and the 15-year olds don't. But in their minds, in their emotional development, in the well-roundedness of their personalities and in the balance of perspective, the difference is not so clear-cut.

Thinking of conscious experience in such black or white terms as 'asleep' or 'awake' is binary thinking. It is limited and lacks maturity. Because nothing in life is binary. Everything exists on a continuum. And this includes consciousness and self.

So, anyone who is communicating to you that they are *awake* is fooling both you and themselves. That is like saying, *I am wholly an adult.* You are not. You are a composite sketch of various stages of development—some further along than others; some unusually evolved, and others stunted. And life is a series of experiences in which we circle back over and over and are made to face and resolve those parts of us still in need of development.

One might say, *Well, I can say I am awake because I no longer feel a sense of being a separate self.*

This is the ultimate self-deception. Because the sense of being a separate self is just an evolutionary mechanism our brains have developed to survive and evolve as a species. You can no more short-circuit that function than you can annihilate your memory. *Everyone* functions with a sense of a separate self to one degree or another. This doesn't mean you are *awake.*

One might say, *Well, my sense of separate self is only intermittent. There are moments where no such separation is felt.*

This is nothing to write home about. In fact, this is what ordinary consciousness looks like. Everybody experiences moments where no such separation is felt. It's just that they are not so hyper-focused on them. Any moment in which you are absorbed in work or sport or music, such separation disappears. Any moment in which one zones out and stares into space, such separation disappears. This doesn't mean you are *awake.*

One might say, *Well, it's more than that. I don't get lost in thoughts and stories about myself like most other people do. My default is to be inwardly silent, thus not feeling a separation.*

Quietude of mind is certainly a therapeutic way to be, but this again is not so unusual. Plenty of people live this way, they're just not talking about it. The vocal ones are the ones suffering the most. This doesn't mean you are *awake.*

One might say, *Well, I no longer harbor beliefs about myself or the world or society. I don't hold religious beliefs, nor beliefs about the nature of reality or the self. I am willing to live in the space of 'I don't know'. I am comfortable with uncertainty.*

This just means you are an intelligent and rational person who doesn't need to modify their view of the world, in order to make it a more conducive place in which to live. There are plenty of intelligent and rational people in the world although they tend to be a rarer breed. This doesn't mean you are *awake.*

One might say, *Well, I no longer think in terms of good or evil. I see the seed of evil in the good and the seed of good in the evil.*

This just means you are someone with a mature perspective who doesn't see people and events in isolation but is able to grasp a big picture view of things. There are many such people with mature vision in the world. This doesn't mean you are *awake.*

One might say, *I no longer identify with my name, my gender, my upbringing, my race, my ethnicity and so on. I don't categorize myself. I just am.*

This just means you are comfortable with being a fluid entity. It means you are more likely to just go with the flow of things. There are many people who similarly go with the flow of things. This doesn't mean you are *awake.*

One might say, *Well, I have had an awakening experience in which I saw how everything is connected. My sense of separation completely disappeared. I saw that everything was of a single existence, a single being.*

This just means you have had a powerful epiphany. Many people from all kinds of religious and non-religious backgrounds have had such experiences. And they explain it in terms of the language that is relevant to the culture from which they have emerged. You call it 'awakening', someone else of Christian faith may call it being 'born again'. Having such an epiphany, no matter how life altering, doesn't mean you are *awake.*

One might say, *I feel a natural outpouring of love for everyone I meet. Each person is another version of myself. I feel a tremendous sense of connection with nature.*

This just means you are a highly empathetic person. Your mirror neurons are firing more rapidly than the average person. Still, there are many who live this way. This doesn't mean you are *awake.*

No matter what you say to qualify your own state of being *awake,* there is someone experiencing ordinary consciousness who experiences the same thing.

So, what does it mean then, to be *awake?*

It means nothing at all.

There are no 'awake' people and 'asleep' people. There is only a continuum of conscious experience where each person will find they land. And even your position on that continuum is not something static. You are moving up and down that spectrum constantly from one moment to the next.

So 'asleep' and 'awake', if we must use those terms, are not two binary positions in which awareness exists, like on and off. Rather they form the two extreme ends of this continuum of conscious experience. Nobody exists at either extreme. In other words, nobody is wholly asleep or wholly awake. We are all continuously moving between the two, with certain individuals tending more towards one extreme than the other.

And it may so happen, that over a lifetime, an individual who tended more towards the asleep end of conscious experiences ends up tending more towards the awake end of conscious experiences. In other words, previously they may have had more acute feelings of separation, more consuming thoughts and emotions, strongly held beliefs, a lot of negative mind momentum and so on. But now they generally tend to experience feelings of separation that are muted, internal quietude, loosely held beliefs and a mellow degree of negativity in the mind.

This still doesn't mean they are *awake*. It just means they have grown into wise and well-balanced adults.

Yet, because this transition over a lifetime from the lower sections of the spectrum to the higher sections feels like such a hero's journey, we want to encapsulate it in a simple-to-understand metaphor. So, we say, *I once was asleep, but now I am awake*. Yet, a metaphor is all it is.

Amazing grace, how sweet the sound
That saved a wretch like me
I once was lost, but now am found
Was blind, but now I see.[34]

It's romantic to think of our journey in this binary way and

34. A Christian hymn published in 1779, with words written in 1772 by the English poet and Anglican clergyman John Newton (1725–1807).

to communicate it to others similarly. But it is not truthful. Because no such flip has happened. All there has been, is a natural evolution of perspective and awareness that still continues as we speak.

Spiritual teachings that promote notions of people as being 'asleep' or 'awake' are no different than the ones of the past that judged us as being good or bad, sinners or saved. They are over-simplifications meant for simpleton minds. Minds that naturally only operate in black and white thinking modes.

But when presented to a mind that sees in many dimensions and hues, such a teaching does great disservice and causes great turmoil. It promises a bag full of goodies or a lump of coal as the only options we have.

Chapter 35
MIRROR, MIRROR

Q: Your posts always bring me back to the simplicity of this moment. You have a way of taking the air out of anything my mind can latch on to. But I still feel burdened by my thoughts. Why does the 'inner world' have to be so complicated when the 'outer one' is so simple? Why are there even two? Why do I need to see myself as a character in my mind? Why can't I *just be* without thinking of myself? Why is there even a mind? I know these are philosophical questions and there are no clear answers. I guess I'm just tied up in confusion…

A: About a year ago, my wife and I were gazing up at a full moon when I remarked, 'Funny, how the phenomenon of tidal locking works. You always get to see the man in the moon.'

To which she responded, 'What man?'

And I said, 'You know. Like the man in the moon. The face in the moon.'

'What face? I don't see a face,' she replied, puzzled.

'What do you mean you don't see a face? Everyone sees a face,' I replied astonished. 'Then what do you see?'

'Nothing in particular. Maybe something like a world map.'

I realized that, having grown up in Eastern Europe, the man in the moon association was not something she had grown up with. Many cultures, in fact, have different versions of what they see. The Japanese, for instance, see a rabbit making *mochi* (glutinous rice).

So, I showed her the man in the moon and it took her a few seconds to see what I was talking about. But then she saw it.

A couple of weeks ago, we were standing on the driveway looking up at the full moon and she goes, 'You know, you've ruined the moon for me. Now, every time I look at the moon all I can see is that ridiculous face!'

Why is There Even a Mind?

Because without one, there would be no form of organization to the reality we perceive. Everything would be as it is: flux. There would be no objects, no events, no people, no space, no time—nothing but incessant emergence, transformation and dissolution. It would be like staring into a cosmic stew. Yet, the mind creates forms out of flux, events out of entropy, people out of phenomena, time out of the timeless, space out of emptiness. Without a mind to organize it, reality would be an incomprehensible soup.

It's like looking up a starry night sky. There was a time when all I saw were incomprehensible clusters of stars. Now when I look up, I see specific constellations. My mind has learned to organize the night sky into a format that makes it more familiar, recognizable and comprehensible.

That is the basic function the mind serves. To organize reality into something that can be interacted with.

But all minds do this. Even the minds of animals.

What makes our human minds different is that we possess the power of imagination. And what that word imagination means is that we are able to simulate scenarios that do not exist in our immediate present. That simulation may take the form of an experience that we are recreating. Or it may take the form of a projected scenario that we may encounter in the future.

Why Simulate at All?

What's the purpose? All this thinking and fantasizing seems to generate a lot of suffering…

The simple reason is that simulation allows for an accelerated evolution.

Think of space travel for instance. Recall when NASA wanted to put a man in outer space? Think of the countless variables and risks they had to consider to achieve that objective. How does zero gravity affect the human body? What kinds of conditions exist in outer space? What temperatures can the external shell of the craft withstand? What kind of heat does the friction of the atmosphere create at speeds that approach escape velocity?

Now, imagine NASA had no simulators. No means of creating similar conditions in the lab to that of outer space. Their astronauts did not spend hours in swimming pools learning to function within low gravity. No one was trained on flight simulators to test every kind of exit and re-entry scenario imaginable. What would have been the odds of success?

If NASA had no choice but to figure it out by trial and error, they would have to build a new space shuttle every single time for every scenario they would need to test. The financial costs of this, not to mention the loss of human life, would be so astronomical that space travel would simply be unviable. Even if they persisted with this approach of trial and error, how many millennia more would it have taken until man could finally enter space?

The mind is the body's simulator.

Its job is to envision multiple scenarios which have either transpired or are yet to transpire and analyze these scenarios in such a way that if any one of them were to ever become a reality, the body would know just what to do in that scenario. It's the same with an airline pilot who uses their training to crash land a plane safely. Obviously they have never had to train on a plane that is actually crashing. But they have simulated these scenarios sufficiently that when it actually happens, their automatic response is one that is suited to the event even if it's the first time they've ever encountered it.

In order to simulate any scenario, the mind has to create a second version of you *in* that simulation. This is your virtual avatar. Your doppelganger. And through each simulation this simulated version of you is going through scenario after scenario: some that end well and some that end badly, even as the 'real you' is sitting in relative comfort and safety. This is like the astronaut who, while sitting in the safety of the NASA lab, is projecting his virtual self into all kinds of dangerous flight-based scenarios.

That virtual version that is the protagonist of the mind's simulations, is what we commonly tend to refer to as 'me'.

Now, none of what I've outlined so far is really the cause of any of our problems. In fact, they are evolutionary mechanisms that have evolved as solutions to the natural challenges that life poses to all organisms.

The problem and root of our existential angst really comes down to two factors:

The first is that the simulations that our minds create are structurally limited. The second is that the simulation is mistaken for reality and thereby the virtual self in the simulation is taken to be the real self.

These two glitches exacerbate each other in a number of ways through an endless feedback loop.

Why Are Some Simulations Flawed?

I'll give you an example. When my daughter was four years old she learned that one puts out a fire by throwing water on it. This made a lot of sense to her, since fire was hot and dry and water was cold and wet. Then one day one of our electrical appliances began sparking and, before I knew it, I saw her running with an empty cup to the sink to fill it with water. So, I stopped her and explained that an electrical fire is different from a regular fire, and water is the one thing that she absolutely should not be using to put it out. Her mind had incorrectly simulated what would happen when she threw that cup of water on the fire. Her imagined scenario had been one in which the fire would have been put out, whereas, in reality, she would have been electrocuted.

The limit of a simulation is that it can only use data with which it is already familiar to project a simulated scenario. All a simulation does is re-organize that data into different permutations and combinations. But it cannot create new data.

That new data only comes from the present moment and our immediate reality. So, either we need to be electrocuted or to know that someone somewhere has been electrocuted in order to understand that one does not throw water on an electrical fire.

So, for example, if you're trying to figure out how to beat traffic to get to work, you may accurately envision a whole number of alternate routes because your mind is already familiar with the layout of the city. Whereas, when you are travelling in a foreign city with no map, your simulations are going to lack data and therefore accuracy.

Thus, the natural stance of a mind needs to be one of data gathering. Rather than actively simulating, it must be actively observing and registering. For a mind to effectively simulate, it must absorb as many data points from its environment as possible in real time. The more keenly observant it is, the more accurate its own simulations are bound to be.

All this is common sense.

However, this is not how most of our minds operate.

Most of our minds are perpetually focused on simulating and only minimally on observing. Rather than actively absorbing data points, they are simply rehashing scenarios based on the limited data they already have.

The mind is limited in its ability to do two things at once. Its attention cannot be fully dedicated to simulating and observing at the same time, so when it is simulating it is barely observing.

Why Do We Compulsively Simulate?

One of the reasons for this tendency to simulate compulsively is what I mentioned earlier. Mistaking the simulated self as the primary self, we have no choice but to favor the simulated reality in the mind as being the fundamental reality we inhabit over the reality our bodies do. And so the entire equation turns backwards.

Rather than adapting our simulations to the physical reality we inhabit, we begin to do the opposite. We try and change physical reality to line up with our simulations. Concurrently, we begin modifying our natural self to match the simulated self.

An extreme example of this is those who compulsively undergo plastic surgery to embody a certain ideal of beauty. It may happen that they end up in creating a distorted and almost inhuman appearance that is a reflection of how distorted their simulated self is in the mind. But even though most of us are not nearly this extreme, almost everyone is doing it to some extent.

Yet, beyond body image, the very choices we make in our lives—where we live, what work we do, what we believe, our political opinions, our self-esteem and so on—all have that same cumulative effect of stuffing a square peg into a round hole. Or in this case, stuffing a self into a me-shaped hole.

What we call the 'ego' is nothing more than a flexible and fluid self, forced into a rigid identity container.

So, this is the fundamental error. This is why most of the suffering we perceive in the world exists. Simulators running amuck, trying to structure reality into whatever distorted hierarchy they are projecting onto it. Our perception has flipped backwards.

Why Has Our Perception Flipped?

Why is there this tendency to mistake the simulated self for the real self in the first place?

Simply put: awareness is attracted to change.

To illustrate what I mean by this, let me tell you about my kids again. In our family, screen time is strongly regulated. The girls get exactly one hour of television in the evenings when they can watch their cartoons. And it's always fascinating to watch them watch their cartoons. Because the moment that TV comes on, they go from being bubbly, enthusiastic kids into absolute zombies.

It is almost impossible to get their attention while they are watching their cartoons. And that's because their awareness favors the TV reality over the reality they are inhabiting, because things are happening at a much faster rate in that reality.

Not much is happening in the living room reality. The cat is stretching and strolling across the carpet. Dad is clearing up some dishes. Mom is setting out the clothes for their school tomorrow. Whereas, in the TV reality, all kinds of amazing, terrifying, exciting things are happening on a moment by moment basis.

In other words, the rate of change in the reality on the screen is much higher than that of the reality around them. And thus, they are fixated on that reality over this one.

This is also why we are so immersed in our own simulated scenarios in the mind over the one we inhabit.

What Kinds of Scenarios Do Our Minds Simulate?

This is a good question to ask. Rarely do we ever simulate mundane scenarios. Most of what we simulate are risk or reward scenarios. In other words, we imagine scenarios in which either good things or bad things are happening to us.

In our minds, we are either getting praised or put down. We are either appreciated or misunderstood. People are either out to get us or love us. We are winning or losing. We are succeeding or failing. We are triumphing or being vanquished. Over and over, these are the kinds of scenarios we are projecting. Because that is the whole point of a simulation. It is to anticipate scenarios of threat or reward in an attempt to maximize our chances of survival.

But it's precisely because these simulations are designed to focus more on the dramatic moments that our awareness is naturally drawn to the simulated reality in preference to the physical one. Dramatic moments cause all sorts of biochemical reactions in our bodies and such biochemicals are addictive. We could be standing in a kitchen making a cup of tea and at the same time be experiencing great grief or joy or terror or heart-warming feelings, based on whatever simulated script is playing out in the mind. This is both miraculous and ominous.

Simulation is stimulation. And when we become addicted to feelings of stimulation (arousal) then we will go looking for more.

Is This Why We Seek Technological Stimulation?

Stimulation seeks greater stimulation.

This is why our rapid technological progress also represents an existential crisis for our species. Because all technology augments the power of the human mind. It magnifies our ability to analyze, organize and simulate.

Yet, precisely because simulation is stimulation, the cumulative effect of this outcome is that levels of stimulation are reaching near critical levels. The addiction is full blown and all consuming.

And since the backwards orientation of our perception

is already a source of suffering, this further technological augmentation creates an exponential increase in that suffering.

The more we simulate, the more versions of our self we create and the more identities we begin to proliferate, the more those identities begin to seem like reality over the simple sense of being. This is more than apparent in the political climate in which most countries of the world are now immersed.

For a mind that is not stable and not grounded in the reality our bodies inhabit, technology is just a plain bad idea. Because it exacerbates every error and magnifies every distortion by several orders of magnitude. Of the 7.8 billion of us, what percentage actually function in a grounded manner? It seems that the majority are completely absorbed in their simulations.

If a child hasn't learned how to ride a bicycle safely, the last thing they need is a motorcycle.

Dominated by a misunderstanding of what this mind is and what we ourselves are, we walk further and further into that labyrinth of simulated realties, further textured and complicated by technology.

The Matrix

And that simulated self remains forever lost in that labyrinth, screaming for a way out.

But there is no way out. Because you were never in.

Mirror, mirror on the wall.

Who is the fairest one of all?

My kids are watching *Snow White* and that familiar refrain from my own childhood causes me to reflect.

Why is the mirror magical? It doesn't seem all that intelligent. If it had been, it would have told the queen something that she did not already have the ability to know. It would have provided her with data that she didn't already possess. It would have told her that beauty is subjective and goes deeper than superficial appearances. But the mirror does not possess any intelligence. So, its own responses are limited by the queen's limited understanding of what beauty is. Thus, it can only give her black or white answers.

Similarly, seeking life, seeking self, seeking solutions to suffering in the mind, is like the queen looking at her magic mirror and asking for solutions. There are simply no solutions to be found because there is no new intelligence there.

What is required is a reorientation of perspective. A return of the natural homeostasis that results when the mind resumes its primary function of observing and data-gathering and only simulating when necessary, as a secondary function.

Yet, that reorientation also cannot be forced. It happens organically with time, understanding and experience. At a certain point, one may simply outgrow the need to constantly stimulate, just like every teen outgrows the need to constantly check their hair in the mirror. When that happens, awareness returns to the reality at hand rather than the simulations being projected.

And the suffering identity in the simulation is seen for the artifice that it is. And the self returns to simply doing what it does best:

Being itself.

Chapter 36

JUST FUCKING LIFE

Q: Dude, I know you're not trying to be a teacher or anything, but I've learned more from reading your articles the last few months than years of listening to spiritual teachers. It makes all this spiritual stuff so clear and simple. Like something has relaxed inside me, you know? It just makes fucking sense. Don't know how else to say it! My question is, why are you the only dude talking about this in this way??? There are a couple of other teachers I know who are critical of the spiritual circus too. But even they are selling some brand of their own 'awake' state. But you've got no skin in the game, man. That's what makes me wanna listen.

A: Why am I the only dude talking about this? I don't know if I am, but if it's true that's a pretty sad state of affairs. You're right, I've got no skin in this game. I've got no skin in any game. Even my everyday jobs that earn me a living are something I can walk away from at a moment's notice if they require me to compromise myself in any way.

I don't live my life seeking external validation in any form, emotional, psychological or financial. The only person whose validation I need is the guy staring back at me in the mirror. And it's not about giving myself props or building up an image of myself either. It's a silent validation. A soundless, *It's all good.*

I trust myself to the extent that I no longer have to think about myself.

I don't know why no one is talking about this. And how simple it all is. I don't know why these gurus are up there ego tripping on the sense of importance they feel when others put them on a pedestal. All I can say is that they must feel utterly terrified inside. Yes, I know about teachers who are critical of the non-dual scene, yet end up manifesting a very similar kind of power dynamic under the guise of it being something else. They're just looking for a new angle from which to market the same old product.

You are the product you're being sold. And like any product, it isn't enough to market just the product. They have to keep providing upgrades, newer models, more features and so on to keep the customer interested and seeking more. It happens in every industry: tech, auto, fashion, business, restaurants—we are constantly reinventing the same things in order to generate an illusion of progress. So, when you are the product, that's what the whole focus is going to be about.

But it's not meant to be that complicated. None of it is that complicated. Complicated is *us*, our minds, what we've turned our lives and ourselves into. But this: life, reality? It's bizarrely simple and straightforward. That's what makes it impossible to accept.

I was chatting with a buddy last night and he goes, 'Man, sometimes I sit on the bench in the park and just look at a tree. And I'll look at it for like an hour or two. I'm not meditating or anything like that. I'm just looking at the tree. And when I'm doing that it just becomes absolutely fucking clear to me that that's all there is to it. That's all the meaning there needs to be. Nothing spiritual or mystical. It's an ordinary tree. Just looking at the fucking tree. It's that simple.'

And I responded, '...and what we call civilization is the sum total of all the infinite techniques human beings have invented in order to avoid looking at that fucking tree.'

Of course, the fucking-tree isn't the point. It could be a fucking-anything. The fucking-mailbox, the fucking-street, the fucking-dog, the fucking-book, the fucking-olympics, the fucking-mailman, the fucking-wife, the fucking-wife fucking the fucking-mailman—you get the idea.

It's just fucking life.

Seeing everything with a simple matter-of-fact awareness requires nothing more to be made of the moment than it already is.

But simplicity is the enemy of progress. If we were just content with looking at the tree, we'd still be living in the jungle along with our other primate cousins who are genuinely content in their tree-gazing.

Yet, some ancestor of ours a bajillion years ago, while looking at that tree, went, 'Nah. There's got to be something more to life than just sitting here looking at this fucking tree.'

So, he went and invented some tools which he used to cut that bastard tree down. Then he cut it up into small blocks and came up with the bright idea to set it on fire. Then he used that fire to burn down entire acres of useless trees. And he planted useful things like 'crops' that served a more functional purpose than simply being stared at. But he couldn't get the fucking tree out of his mind even though he had already assassinated it and its entire extended family.

So, he began to dig into the ground and discovered that the dead fucking-tree, along with other dead things, had turned into fucking-coal and fucking-oil. So, he invented machines that could use these dead tree-corpses to build massive steel and concrete cities in which not a single structure he built looked anything like a tree. In fact, they were designed to be distinctly anti-tree-like.

And living in his concrete bubble, he invented things like politics and religion, government and law, culture and tradition, technology and fashion, science and medicine and so on: infinite ways in which to preoccupy himself in an effort to prove the correctness of his original declaration, 'There's got to be something more to life than just sitting here looking at this fucking tree.'

But there was something missing. Something gnawing at him on the inside. He was unhappy. Even though he was more comfortable than he had ever been in the jungle, even though he had literally doubled his life expectancy—that increase in quantity had not translated into an increase in quality. If anything the quality had deteriorated. At the back of his mind, he had this niggling sense that that 'something missing' had to do with the fucking-tree. Over time, he came to accept the fact that he needed to look at it again. But how?

So, he began to invent spiritual practices that would teach him how to look at the fucking-tree properly. And he began to seek the counsel of expert tree-gazers, those who claimed to have transcended all desire to look-away-from-trees. Those who claimed to have realized their own tree-nature.

He paid a lot of money to these good, magnanimous folks. A lot of fucking-trees died in order to print all that cash he paid to those good teachers. And they taught him to feel all kinds of things about trees. They taught him to worship them. To offer sacrifices to them. To be filled with ecstasy, love and bliss at the very thought of them. To see his own tree-nature.

He began to dress in only bark and leaves. He would meditate while standing and holding his arms upwards pretending to be a tree. He studied botany and could list every single species of tree that existed. He would meet with his other tree-loving friends and together they would spend hours talking about the beauty and freedom of trees. They would all join hands and sway together like the branches of a tree in the wind.

Yet as the years passed on he began to realize that he still felt empty. That all his worship and seeking hadn't filled that void inside him. He was still missing something. And it still had to do with that fucking-tree…

Then one day, depressed and confused, he walks down to a park. And he sits down, next to this other guy who seems relaxed and passively gazing at something. He asks the guy what he is looking at and the guy responds, 'a tree.'

And our friend embarks on this long monologue about what trees are, what tree-nature is, the millions of species of trees, the importance of trees in our lives, the benefits of tree-gazing, the greatest tree-gazing gurus he has had the fortune of studying under, his mystical experiences of union with trees and the sudden realization of his own tree-nature.

And the guy on the bench is just passively nodding, 'Uh huh, uh huh', while continuing to look at the tree.

And our friend, a bit peeved by this guy's lack of acknowledgement of his own knowledge, expertise and realization begins to berate him as being superficial for not having delved deeply enough into the matter. He tells him that there are layers and layers of reality within trees. That the guy is blindly living in a concrete Matrix designed to prevent him from recognizing his own tree-nature. And that there is more to this existence than meets the eye.

The guy on the bench continues nodding passively, unfazed and uninterested. Our friend becomes quite disturbed at this point. He inquires how the guy is so unconcerned. Isn't the guy interested in what this whole thing called life is all about? Isn't he interested in discovering the deeper purpose and meaning behind it all? The guy shakes his head without looking away.

At this point, our friend breaks down and confesses that he is lost. That he has searched high and low for a solution to his suffering. That he has done everything possible to try and acknowledge the fucking-tree: he has studied about it, meditated on it, sung songs of devotion to it, tried to become one with it, tried to surrender to it, tried to make love to it—but nothing has worked. He still feels a tree-shaped void inside his heart. Is there anything, anything at all the guy could offer him in the form of a pointer or some advice that will help him on his quest? He has suffered in his doubt and confusion for so long!

Just a word! Even a single word that will shine even one ray of light into the darkness of his own existence!

The guy on the bench sighs and turns to him and goes:

'Bro, shut the fuck up and just look at the fucking tree.'

Chapter 37
SECRETS OF THE UNIVERSE

Q: Do you mean to tell me that there are no words of wisdom that are of any value to you? There is no teacher whom you would consider worthy of listening to?

A: That's not true.

Around midnight last night, I cracked open a can of beer, sat on the steps outside my front door and listened to the trees for the better part of an hour. They have more wisdom than any human being is capable of. Attending a satsang with the trees, so much is revealed. If you hear any wisdom from me it's merely a regurgitation of what they have spoken to me in their own fluid language, translated into the crude and clumsy jargon that humans use.

But it's a different ear with which the wisdom of the trees needs to be listened to. There can be no anticipating what they are going to say next. They do not speak in sentences. Their thoughts don't end predictably, the way our human ones do.

Human language is like listening to pop music. Once you've heard the first verse and the chorus of the song, your mind already knows what the rest of the song is going to sound like. It's mostly repetitive. But the sound of the trees is like a symphony composed in real-time. The only way one can listen is if one is completely without any sense of expectation or anticipation. Any expectation is sure to be met with disappointment because what you hear is impossible to predict.

The language of the trees is a remarkable language. Silence is as much a part of their vocabulary as is sound. And when they speak, I feel their breath ruffling through my hair, caressing my skin, awakening my senses. And then silence again. Indefinitely. As my consciousness marinates in what has been said.

Human teachers are like rudimentary instruments. They are like a toy piano only capable of basic sounds and notes that are amusing at best and tinny at worst. They regurgitate the same tired notes with uninspiring variations that try their best to sound original but ultimately amount to nothing more than chewing the intellectual cud.

But when the trees speak, every syllable uttered is conceived, created and uttered for the very first time. If you know how to listen, the teaching is evergreen. Perennially fresh. Not a word regurgitated. Not a thought repeated. Not an ounce of energy wasted on communicating anything but the direct and absolute truth.

When I have the trees as my teachers—to hold satsang whenever my heart desires, whenever my soul requires nourishment, why would I turn to a human being? Why would I reject the real deal and opt for the cheap knockoff?

What you call a 'teacher' I call a 'translator'. That's all these human teachers are. Middlemen with varying levels of translating skills. Most of them are simply just making shit up as they go because they don't really understand what is being communicated to them by life.

But even if they did? So what? Why listen to their tinny voices? Their limited notes? Their predictable and regurgitated thoughts? Why listen to a shitty scratched up CD when you have an open seat to the live concert?

Makes no sense to me.

The trees have been my teachers for the better part of two decades now. They have always accepted me as an equal in their midst. They have never made me feel lower than them even though they tower over me. They have always displayed great humility even though they are the most majestic creatures I've ever met. They have watched me in my despair, in my epiphanies, in my anguish and my happiness. They have watched me nearly kill myself. And through it all they have always spoken kindly, chided me gently, met my arrogance with stony silence, advised me in my confusion and responded to my courage with rustling enthusiasm.

They have been my friends first, before they have been my teachers. I trust them more than I do my own loved ones. Isn't that what every seeker is in search of in a teacher?

No human can give me that. We humans are merely sophisticated mouthpieces. Our words are the brutal sounds of a hammer mauling a brick wall. 'Well, some humans create beauty with words,' you may argue. And some people make music using hammers—yet, there are much finer instruments one can use to create music than hammers.

I can never aspire to be a teacher of wisdom. Because I know what I am.

I am a poor translator. I am a redundant middleman. I am a sophisticated mouthpiece. I am a regurgitator of unoriginal and predictable thoughts. I am a cheap knockoff.

Yet, when I listen to the trees I become something more. Or rather, something less.

When they speak to me, I become a child. No. Not even a child, a mere newborn.

I know nothing. I understand nothing. I anticipate nothing. I become nothing.

And in that nothing, the secrets of the universe are revealed to me.

Chapter 38

AN IMPOSSIBLE CHOICE

Q: There's a dilemma I'm having that I'm hoping you can shed some light on. I've been with this teacher for some time. He is one of the most brilliant people I've met. I've been sensing many disturbing things about him. The way he treats people doesn't match up with his 'state of realization'. I'm starting to think he is full of it. I tried to address this with him once and he became quite aggressive. Some of the members in our community began to turn on me. I'm having a really hard time with this. I think I can see through his mask now. But at the same time many of my friends still believe in him. I don't want to lose them. So, I still play nice. But it doesn't feel right to me. I feel I'm being faced with an impossible choice. I'm not sure what I should do...

A: I'm not sure what you should do either. But let me tell you a little story about Mr. Welcome...

When I was in the 5th grade I attended an all-boys British school in Kolkata (Calcutta, at that time). Our class teacher was a man named Mr. Welcome.

Mr. Welcome was one of those teachers you dreamed of having. He was good looking, oozed machismo and was incredibly charismatic. He was an excellent teacher. He kept his students' attention hanging off his every word. He was hilarious, inspirational and magnetic. He made every one of us feel like we were part of his team. He called us his 'boys' and he felt more like a father to us than our own fathers were. Our class was the envy of other classes. Most other boys wished they had Welcome as their class teacher.

If the picture is still unclear to you, I want you to envision Robin Williams in the movie *Dead Poets Society* and the famous scene where Walt Whitman's poem 'O Captain, My Captain!'[35] was recited by all the class. Mr. Welcome was our captain. And we were his troops. I'm quite sure any of us would have gone to war for him, that's how much we loved and believed in him. That is how much love we felt from him as well.

And of all the boys in class, I was his golden boy. He often told me I reminded him of himself when he was my age. I was an excellent English student (the subject he primarily taught). I could quote writers ranging from Shakespeare to P. G. Wodehouse back to him. I was a fierce scrapper and competitive in sports. He had been a boxer and a track athlete as well in his youth. I loved him like he was my own father.

Every year, the school held an elocution contest. This was an oratory event in which contestants could choose a poem or a piece of prose and recite it to an audience and a panel of judges. Each class from every grade put forth one or two contestants for the contest. Because of my sharp oratory skills, I was selected to take part in the event that year. I had chosen a particularly humorous story—a poem by Roald Dahl—for my piece. I spent two months rehearsing it in preparation for the event.

A couple of weeks before the event, Mr. Welcome announced to the class that the school had come up with a new event: a dramatics contest which would occur in only a week's time. Each class would have to put on a play and the winning class would win a field trip somewhere special. The news electrified the class and everyone immediately began wondering what play we would put on. How could we create a script at such short notice? Who would the actors be? How would we learn our lines so quickly?

35. 'O Captain, My Captain!' Whitman, Walt. 1865. *Leaves of Grass.*

Mr. Welcome then announced to the class that he had decided that the play our class would perform, was the same story I was reciting for the elocution contest. He said it was an excellent and humorous story and, since we were all familiar with it after watching me rehearse it, it would be a story everyone could ramp up on quickly. Then he looked at me and flashed one of his charming smiles,

'You don't mind, do you, my boy?'

I was a bit surprised by his decision, especially since performing it just a week before my own contest would take the element of surprise out of my own performance. But I didn't think twice about it. I wanted our class to win no matter the cost. I grinned back and said it was no problem at all.

'That's my boy!'

That evening I mentioned to my mother that our class would be putting on a play. When she asked what play it was, I told her it was the same one I would be reciting a week later. She was taken aback by this. 'Why would he choose that particular play when he knows how hard you've been working on this?' she asked. I told her it wasn't a big deal. And she insisted it was. She said she was going to write a letter to him explaining the conflict of interest. I said it wasn't necessary, but she reassured me that she was going to say it very nicely and even recommend some alternative scripts that she would be happy to type out for him. Eventually, her insistence wore me down and I caved.

The next morning I delivered the letter to Mr. Welcome as the class assembled. We all took our seats as he stood silently reading the letter. I watched him intently and started to get this uneasy knot of anxiety in my stomach. Something didn't feel right. His face darkened. He didn't look at me. He simply placed the envelope on the table and said to the class:

'I have an announcement to make.'

It sounded so serious, everyone hushed at once. That knot in my stomach was now a sick feeling.

'My boys, we have been let down by one of our own. Someone we trusted. Someone I believed in more than I've believed in any other. He has betrayed us. Shiv doesn't want our class to succeed. He only cares about himself. He only cares about winning for himself. He has been a coward. He has made his mother write a letter to tell me what I can or can't do. He has taken our play away from us. That's right, boys. We are no longer allowed to do it. But don't worry—we will find something else. We will find a way to succeed despite his act of cowardice and betrayal. Let this be a lesson, boys! Even a trusted brother can suddenly stab you in the back if he stands to benefit. Now we all know his true colors.'

I couldn't believe what I was hearing. It was as if time stood still in that moment. I watched the entire image I had built of the man in my mind shatter into a million pieces. I could feel the fiery glance of 39 other boys searing into the back of my neck. I went from class hero to social pariah in a single instant.

'What do you have to say for yourself?' The words echoed in the background rousing me from my stupor. Mr. Welcome was glaring at me. I knew what he wanted. What he needed.

I stood up to address him, as was customary, and replied, my voice shaking, 'I have nothing to say. I stand by that letter.'

His eyes grew wide with disbelief. He had fully expected me to grovel, to repent, to beg forgiveness, to confess that I had made a momentary and fatal error, to be begged to be let back in the fold. He would have, in his usual charming way, magnanimously forgiven me and told me not to give into my petty vanity at the expense of my brotherhood ever again, or some such nonsense. Yet, none of that held any appeal for me anymore. In that single instant, I saw through him and the sham of a 'brotherhood' that we were.

The class went ahead and put on a different play the following week. The play had 39 participants. I was the only one excluded from participating, by Mr. Welcome himself.

For the remainder of the year he made my life hell. He graded me more unforgivingly than he did the other boys. My efforts to participate in the classes were completely ignored. He often made remarks to humiliate or ridicule me in front of the other boys. And they all lapped it up and laughed and guffawed. They called me 'weak', a 'coward', a 'loser', a 'traitor', a 'sellout', a 'snake'. It stung badly, of course. These had all been my friends, my brothers. Now, I was worse than scum to them.

But I never regretted my decision: not to acquiesce... not to compromise my own self-respect in order to win back their love.

The year went by.

It was the last week of class. And by now, Welcome's attitude towards me had begun to soften a bit. I sensed that he felt I had been in purgatory long enough. So, he asked me to stand up in class one day. And he looked at me with his usual charming smile and said:

'I think he's learned his lesson now, eh, boys? What do you say, Shiv? Shall we say this has been an important learning experience for everyone and put it past us, my boy?' The others were all murmuring. They seemed happy at this final reconciliation at the end of the school year.

He was looking at me with that twinkle in his eye, that roguish smile. I felt a slight tug within me—a reminder of what used to be.

And then I looked him dead straight in the eyes and said:

'I'm not your boy.'

Welcome stared at me, still smiling. The other boys were shocked. He nodded, then looked away and continued with the class.

Even after I went to the 6th grade, I'd sometimes encounter him in the hallways. He'd make some friendly remark, try to engage me in some sportive kind of way. But I wouldn't give him the time of day. I knew what he was. And I knew what I was...

***

The dynamic you are referring to isn't exclusive to spiritual circles. It exists everywhere: in schools, in corporations, in the military—you name it. The strength of the herd and the sense of belonging one feels, especially when under the guidance of a charismatic leader, is a powerful force. It's powerful enough to start wars and revolutions.

But there is one thing that is even more powerful than that. And that is the power of your own spirit. It is infinitely more powerful.

But there is no way for you to *really know* this until you have put it to the test. And such tests come in the form of making impossible choices. Choices that feel like burning every bridge we have built and excommunicating ourselves from the ones we know and love. No wonder few ever make such choices.

I have known incredible, conscientious, kind people stand by and watch abuse and discrimination happen because they were faced with this impossible choice. I have watched strong, independent and self-respecting people accept abuse and comply with conditions that go against their own sense of ethics because they were faced with this impossible choice.

I cannot tell you what you need to do. I can only tell you what I did. And that wasn't the only time I stood up to a false authority in my life. I did it over and over and over again. And each time, without fail, I was alienated from my clan as a result of it.

Yet, in the end, each alienation just served to set me more in tune with myself.

Each excommunication from a foreign land I once believed was my own, only served to deliver me closer to home.

The world is full of Mr. Welcomes. But there is only one of you. The real choice you face is which one you will choose to honor.

Chapter 39
SPIRITUAL CONSUMERISM

Q: So do you think human beings don't need guidance? It's every man or woman to fend for themselves? This doesn't resonate with me. To me, gurus and teachers play a crucial role in society...

A: No, I can't say human beings don't need guidance. Guidance can be crucial at certain points in a human being's development. But guidance, by its very nature, is a double-edged sword. And depending on how it is approached, it will either provide just the right kind of support that the person needs or it will hamper an individual's development.

If you look at a parent-child relationship, it is a guidance-based relationship. As a dad, I guide my daughters at various points of their development, but I have to be careful not to become too involved. If there is too little guidance, they will flounder. If there is too much they will develop an over-reliance on me and won't learn to trust their own strengths and competencies.

When I guide my children, they always know that they can rely on me if things go south, yet they never feel like they can remain in their comfort zones around me. They know full well, Dad is going to push them just that extra bit past where they like to be. Many parents from my generation tend towards the over-protective end of the spectrum. They are almost pathologically involved in their children's lives, guiding and keeping watch over them 24/7. This kind of guidance often backfires to result in a stunted emotional and psychological development of the self.

Next year, my older daughter goes to 1st grade. And she will have to walk over a mile to school on her own with no parents accompanying her. Japan is one of the few countries in the world where this is still possible and even required. It's one of the factors that led to me moving here. Children here exhibit an independence from their parents that is virtually non-existent in our hyper-involved western societies. Both my wife and I enjoyed that sort of independence when we were children. It is what has made us the self-determined adults we are. It's something that we wanted our kids to experience also.

The reason I appear to take such a hard stance against gurus and spiritual teachers is because the culture in which these individuals thrive has a warped idea of what 'guidance' is about. They are not interested in empowering seekers, they are interested in developing an over-reliance on themselves. I know parents who are like this too. They want their kids close to them always, so they pander to their needs and keep them emotionally under-developed and always dependent upon them.

Very few of these so called 'teachers' are in the business because they are genuinely interested in contributing something. Most are in it to gain something—fame, popularity, power, authority, adoration, money, stature and so on. Even the ones who don't have such high ambitions eventually get drawn into it, because the culture itself requires it. The world of spiritual seeking is practically infested with emotionally traumatized seekers who claim to desire truth, but really only want their wounds to be soothed.

Soothing isn't guidance.

When my daughter took off her training wheels aged five and fell and scraped her knee, I held her and comforted her for all of 15 seconds and then told her that she needed to get back on. After that, I watched her get on that bike, even though she was afraid to, and try again. Within minutes she was laughing madly—not because I had soothed her, but because she had conquered her own fear and mastered that bike.

Popular spirituality today is comprised of comforting, soothing, feel-good rhetoric designed to keep seekers firmly fixed within their comfort zones and stunted in their development. That is why people keep seeking for so many years—even decades. They were never pushed into that uncomfortable space and encouraged to negotiate it on their own terms.

It's precisely because spiritual guidance is a business, rather than a form of education, that this happens.

In the business world, customer *retention* is a marker of success whereas *turnover* is a sign that your product isn't in high demand. So, Apple, for example, has built a huge base of loyal customers who swear by Apple products and buy nothing else. It's such customers (and not the one-off buyers) who make Apple a successful company. They are Apple's primary stakeholders.

In the education model, however, it is the opposite. Turnover is a marker of success and retention is a sign that the quality of education offered is substandard. As a high school teacher, I can testify that if even one of my kids was flunking class and repeating the year, it would reflect *very* badly on my skills as a teacher. I'd have to answer to the administration for mere retention, no matter how good a job I think I'm doing.

But you look at the world of spiritual teaching—suddenly things look wonky.

If these gurus are really here to guide us, then according to the education model they must be doing an atrocious job of it. Year after year, the same students keep repeating class and almost no one ever graduates! If a college or university had that sort of abysmal record, no one would ever apply to it.

However, if they are indeed following the business model then they are misrepresenting themselves as our teachers and guides. They are *businessmen* and *women* and we are their customers. And if you understand that, you will see how so-called 'guidance' can't really be a priority here. To create a high turnover in one's customers is plain bad for business.

So, you gotta pick.

If this is a business, which is perfectly fine, just don't misrepresent what you are and why you're doing it. Steve Jobs didn't create Apple to help people, he did it to make money. Don't call yourself a guru or a teacher. Call yourself an 'existential consultant' or a 'spiritual entrepreneur'.

Or if this is primarily about guidance, then your focus needs to be about getting students out of the door just as fast as they come in through it! There is absolutely no excuse for them to be sitting at your feet, year after year, creating groups and communities and Sunday afternoon *satsangs* around your teachings.

If the size of your alumni-population isn't significantly larger than the number of students currently enrolled with you: You are a terrible guide.

Guidance is most effective when it is short and sweet. It comes into an individual's life right when they are at a crossroads, it adds the weight of experience and insight to the one side that the person is already leaning towards but is second guessing themselves on. And then as the person takes their first step onto that new path, whoosh! The guidance is gone. Completely retracted. Leaving the individual to figure it out on their own two feet ... now.

To everyone who reads my stuff, I say the same thing too:

> *Stick around for only as long as required but not a moment longer. Even the words on this page, if read for too long, will just become another crutch and take you to a comfort zone in which you may end up languishing for the next chunk of your life. I don't need any squatters.*

So, to sum up. I do agree that guidance can be key, when provided by competent mentors with the right intentions in mind. However, in the current spiritual climate, I seldom see either competency or right intentions driving the teachings out there. Most of what I see is a whole lot of hype and very little substance:

Superficiality parading as 'depth'...

Narcissism parading as 'expertise'...

Propaganda parading as 'empowerment'...

Greed and power-hungriness parading as 'goodwill and guidance'...

In reality, this culture isn't about guidance. It's about spiritual consumerism.

Chapter 40

STAYING ALIVE

I'm going to try and lay this down as simply as I can:

That spiritual 'enlightenment' you're searching for? Not gonna happen.

No matter what you do, no matter how hard you try, no matter what you are willing to endure, no matter how much you sacrifice yourself in the hopes of one day waking up—every ounce of that effort is literally what is preventing you from seeing what is right in front of your eyes.

This ideal of the awakened being, the enlightened one, is an ideological poison that has infected so many brains and completely hijacked their functioning.

Now, I get why it's so appealing. Society has done us no favors. Its excessive focus on wealth over wisdom, on progress over presence, on consumption over compassion, on success over self-knowledge has led to a horrid state of affairs in which we are alienated from one another and especially from ourselves. We find ourselves in a dull, gray haze of meaninglessness that immediately wilts every form of life it comes upon.

Then, in the midst of such desolation, along comes a spiritual teaching that promises the exact opposite. It promises ecstatic bliss, boundless love for one another and ourselves, a feeling of oneness with all that exists, no more fear of the narrow self-interested ego. We begin to greet others with heartfelt hugs and namastes rather than rough handshakes or polite bows. We begin to lose ourselves in songs of devotion and rhythmic drum circles under starlit skies and to the sounds of the waves lapping on the shore. We feel effusive love for everyone we meet and see the same reflected back in their eyes. And it seems we have finally found our home and our kin. We have left that gray miserable world behind and emerged into a parallel universe bursting with color, love and truth.

For a time.

Yet, unexpectedly, the old feelings of grayness begin seeping back in. At first we try and rationalize them away as just having a bad day. But then it happens more often. Our interactions begin to lack the luster they had before. We continue to participate in the devotional songs, the drum circles, yet it feels a bit contrived. We continue to greet one another with hugs and namastes but we also see how these shows of affection are somewhat superficial. We begin to see through others and the facades they are projecting because they are similar to the ones we ourselves are projecting. We begin to see the grayness lurking behind their eyes, the fear behind their smiles, the quiet desperation with which they sing their songs of devotion, the anxiety concealed in every beat of the drum.

Spirituality is the art of pretending things are okay when they are not.

The more tormented a person is, the more complex the cover-up. We will do everything in our power to surround ourselves with the things, the people, the teachings and the rituals that allow us to maintain that active state of denial in the most comprehensive manner possible. And when we ourselves are the problem then we will seek to deny our selves altogether. That's what the appeal of non-duality is. Escape from the self. Total escape.

Some spiritual seekers are among the most emotionally damaged and psychologically wounded people one will ever meet. And there is a reason why a lofty goal such as 'enlightenment' appeals to such a person. The solution is in proportion to the problem perceived. And nothing short of a complete overhaul of who we are will suffice to solve it.

This was the rationale feeding the mind of one of my readers before he shot himself a couple of days ago. I had never had the opportunity to interact with him directly but I noticed he liked a few of my posts online. I was informed of his death by his best friend who is also an active reader and with whom I have had a fair amount of interaction. He messaged me with the news because this is exactly the sort of thinking I have been criticizing through my writings on this page.

What I felt last night when I heard what had happened was a mixture of deep sadness and rage. I barely slept because the image of this boy, who felt compelled to throw his life away because he couldn't awaken, kept haunting my thoughts. Believing himself to be a failure in life, that sense of failure was further compounded by his 'spiritual failure' to awaken.

As a result of all the enlightenment propaganda he'd come to believe in, he became convinced that if he could only become awakened, like all his teachers seemed to be, his life would become radically different. That all his problems would go away.

He suffered long with depression, headaches, insomnia and ringing in his ears. But when his friend counselled him to seek help he refused. He chose instead to believe what the brainwashed neophytes of the New Age were echoing around him: that all these were signs of awakening...

What a fucking tragedy.

Spiritual propaganda is just another ideological poison, just another narcotic which may help you wean off the drug of materialism that most other people are hooked on to, but in the end will consume you from the inside and leave you a spectre of your former self.

'Waking up' has nothing to do with any of this non-dual garbage that people are being fed about transcending the self, these idiotic songs of devotion sung to some invisible entity who doesn't give a fuck about the singers. It is simply taking a look at what's around right now and choosing to take responsibility for that over anything else the mind can envision as a better reality.

And 'what's around' includes the debts, the relationship woes, the conflict with family, the self-doubt, the uncertainty about the future—all those things that we are attempting to escape using convoluted spiritual practices.

It also means that we are not seeking to define ourselves in either material or spiritual terms. There is no 'success' and 'failure', no 'loser' or 'winner' in anything we choose to do in our lives. Some things we choose will hurt more than others. But that is all part of the learning process by which we calibrate our own responses.

Nature has programmed us with one job, which is to stay alive. Even the amoeba understands this. The only failure is the premature ending of that process.

I'm fed up of this fucking bullshittery. A spiritual circus act with these larger-than-life troupes of performers led by greedy, disingenuous ringmasters fleecing their audiences for every ounce of material and spiritual wealth they possess. And the gullible sheep who will willingly swallow whatever shit they are being fed because they are so used to being led out to pasture.

So, let me lay down some truths right now so that anyone who is thinking of walking down that road may have a moment to pause.

> 1. There is no such thing as an awakened or enlightened person. No such permanent state of consciousness exists. Everyone who has ever existed including the Buddha, Ramana, Nisargadatta and all the other enlightened people inhabit the same everyday ordinary kind of consciousness as do you and I and all the other average joes.
>
> 2. Some people have awakening or *satori* experiences which are temporary spiritual epiphanies. Sudden

moments of clarity in which things appear to come together in a way that they previously hadn't. Nobody lives in a state of constant epiphany. Every epiphany, every insight, every heightened state of consciousness must eventually subside and give way to ordinary consciousness.

3. There is absolutely no way to intentionally and accurately orchestrate such an awakening experience. Trying to do so is an effort in futility and a surefire recipe for great suffering.

4. Rarely, an awakening experience may follow a catastrophic 'nervous breakdown' or a period of intense depression. But depression is not a symptom of awakening, although it may mean that you should seek professional help! (Just because some people emerge from car crashes with a new zest for life doesn't mean car crashes are events one must glorify or aspire to experience.)

5. Ordinary consciousness *is* where the marrow of life exists.

6. No matter how many epiphanies one has had, one's problems cannot simply vanish. They must be faced. And we must take responsibility for them. Such problems must be solved by oneself and no one else. Otherwise, they simply remain and magnify over time.

7. Whatever you resist, persists. Whatever you suppress, festers. Whatever you deny, grows in the darkness of your ignorance.

8. If you truly are willing to take full responsibility for life as it is, rather than as you wish it to be, you will find that all the tools you need to fulfill that responsibility are at your disposal.

9. Nothing is worth ending your life over. No suffering is too great, no hardship too difficult to endure. The human spirit is equipped with a power and an endurance that is truly supernatural. There is only one thing that can subvert it and that is *ideology*: that is our kryptonite.

10. A single ordinary moment of being alive is the highest spiritual achievement anyone can aspire to.

Allow all of this to really sink in. Forget what you've been taught by society. Forget all the dreams and promises you've been fed by your gurus. Watch the edifices of materialism and spirituality crumble before your eyes. Take a stand and say: *Never again*!

Chapter 41

THE NEED OF THE HOUR

When I was in my twenties, I organized a Philosophy Meetup Group in Toronto. We were about five to six members who would meet up once a week and discuss the existential questions of life over a cup of coffee. One of these members, was a woman who was in her fifties at the time. Her name was Kathy.

Kathy was an intelligent woman, with a wisdom that was quite evident the moment you met her. She and I hit it off immediately and often, even after the group would disperse, the two of us would linger and be passionately immersed in conversation on whatever topic struck our fancy. We were fascinated by each other's minds.

Kathy had had a rough childhood. She grew up in the Canadian foster care system. She moved a total of seven times between the ages of three and sixteen. She would talk about how awful the conditions in some of the homes were. One set of foster parents were drug addicts and they would use the welfare money that they received from the government for her care, to shoot up. She and her foster siblings were forced to fend for themselves.

At another home, she was molested by her foster dad while her foster mom watched. When she told her foster sister about it, her sister confessed that the same had happened to her and the girl before her, who had ended up taking her own life soon after leaving foster care. Eventually, these foster parents were charged and Kathy was moved to another home.

Here, Kathy had a somewhat normal life but her parents

were aloof. It was clear that this was just a business transaction for them. The only real family she had was a grandmother who loved her dearly but was unable to care for her because she lived in an assisted living facility. Visits with her grandma would fill her up with love and give her the strength to return to those horrible homes she lived in.

Eventually, Kathy became an adult. She was extremely bright so she went to college. But she ended up doing drugs. She entered bad relationship after bad relationship with men who mistreated her and abused her. Eventually, she evolved past all of that.

When I met her, Kathy had a lightness about her. She seemed a genuinely happy person. Which is why hearing about her past was a shock to me. She confessed to me that, in hindsight, she was glad that all of that had happened. Every bit of pain, misery, suffering and abuse she had experienced had brought her to the awareness and understanding that she now had. All the good and all the bad had contributed to her growth and learning. How could it have happened any other way?

Yet, Kathy was also a vocal advocate for reforming the Canadian foster care system. She frequently campaigned and lobbied for policy changes to be made in the administration of foster care and the screening of potential foster parents. She worked closely with grassroots organizations to make changes at the very ground level. She worked to get kids out of abusive homes. She told me that the system was perverse and that abuse was systemic because of the very fundamentals upon which the structure was based…

Upon hearing her deep acceptance of her own past and experience within foster care versus her passionate resistance and activism against the foster care system—my twenty-year-old mind found this confusing and paradoxical. How can one have acceptance and yet show resistance at the same time?

I was yet to learn to grasp the paradoxical nature of wisdom. It would take me another decade to see the world the way

Kathy did…

It's been a repeating objection that many readers have had to my articles where I am critical of spiritual culture and spiritual teachers in general. The argument many of these well-meaning readers propose is:

Well, I have learned a lot from both the positive and negative experiences that I've had. I've had good gurus and fake gurus and both have had something to teach me. So I don't see why one needs to be critical of the industry. Good or fake, there is something to learn from all of them.

This is the argument. It is a confused argument and I'm going to illustrate why.

As I mentioned earlier, my friend Kathy had developed a deep acceptance of all that had happened to her in foster care. She had learned much from the abuse, the neglect, the assault and also from the love she received from her grandma. So, as far as she was concerned, the rotten foster parents had played a vital role in her own growth as an individual.

However, this did not stop her from being critical of the foster care system and becoming a vocal advocate for reform. She didn't just say, *Well, there are some good parents too, you know. Not all are bad. And the bad ones also have something to teach us, so there is no use being critical of the foster care system.*

And there is a reason she didn't resort to this kind of thinking which is something that plagues most spiritual seekers and teachers today. And that is because she understood that there are two kinds of wisdom.

Philosophical Wisdom Vs. Practical Wisdom

Philosophical wisdom can be considered the 'wisdom of being'.

In other words, philosophical wisdom has to do with an acceptance of things as they are. Philosophical wisdom attempts to zoom all the way out to the 30,000 foot view of life and take all the myriad factors and variables that contribute to the events that happen. It tries to grasp the complex interrelationship of causes and effects and thus attempts to reserve judgment on what is good and bad, right and wrong. It attempts, instead, to establish a holistic view of life and operate from there.

Philosophical wisdom is a critical ingredient of hindsight.

In fact, if we have not learned to develop a holistic attitude towards our own past, it is quite likely that the past is still a sticking point and continues to traumatize us in some way. Having a holistic view of the past means viewing all the positive and negative events of one's life as the singularly propelling 'coupling force' that has contributed to our evolution as individuals. This is both a psychologically healthy and wise perspective to maintain.

However, there is also this thing called *practical wisdom*. And practical wisdom can be considered the 'wisdom of action'.

That action could look like anything: acceptance, resistance, encouragement, discouragement, agreement, disagreement, complimenting, critiquing and so on. Practical wisdom zooms all the way in to the 'ground level view' of life and sets its coordinates using only a few parameters in its environment. It operates with a strong judgment to navigate efficiently and effectively forward. Good, bad, right, wrong in this case have to be very clear cut as we move forward in this perspective. It operates on a dualistic evaluation of its environment, rather than an holistic view.

Practical wisdom is a critical ingredient of foresight. If we have not developed practical wisdom we are likely to feel indecisive about how to act when faced with the often complex and conflicting circumstances of life. Practical wisdom is essential for us to develop an ethical standard of living. It allows for little ambiguity about what is acceptable or unacceptable in terms of circumstances it encounters. It is extremely clear cut and common-sensical in nature.

The Confusion

The problem is that philosophical wisdom and practical wisdom cannot operate exclusively. They must operate in tandem if there is to be a balance of being and action within the organism.

And if you look at society, you will see two kinds of imbalance.

Most of what we call 'material society' operates purely from the standpoint of practical wisdom. In other words, there are very pragmatic guidelines laid down for them as they go about their lives. However, because such guidelines lack philosophical wisdom, they apply practical wisdom to their hindsight.

And this is where they err. Because they treat their past as they would their future—as something that could have or should have been different. Thus, there is no acceptance. This lack of acceptance causes them much suffering.

On the other hand, most of what we might call 'spiritual society' is operating primarily from the standpoint of philosophical wisdom. In other words, they are applying a holistic lens to everything as they go about their days. The problem arises when they apply that same philosophical wisdom to their foresight.

And this is where they err. Because they treat their futures as they would their past—as something that already *is* and can't be any different—in other words it is inevitable. Thus, there is no impulse for action. Because when acceptance is already the case, what is the motivation to change anything?

The only way to offset either kind of bias is to *live the paradox*.

The spiritual industry has propagated systemic abuse, neglect, exploitation and subjugation for centuries because of this very phenomenon of philosophizing heinous acts as being teachable moments. When taken to the extreme (and this is not uncommon amongst seekers in some cults) we actually rationalize the bad behavior and abuse by a teacher as a 'mark of their enlightenment'.

When the famous teacher Chögyam Trungpa[36] had his bodyguards forcibly drag the US Poet Laureate, W.S.Merwin, and his girlfriend, Dana Naone, from their room and held them down and stripped them naked in front of a crowd of onlookers, his students hailed his brand of teaching as 'Crazy Wisdom'. When Sogyal Rinpoche,[37] endorsed by the Dalai Lama to spread Buddhism in the west, punched a young female devotee in the stomach on stage because she hadn't understood what he said, no one came to her aid. For decades, his followers simply accepted his bad behavior because they believed there was much to learn from how 'triggered' they felt by it.

When we are too philosophical about the future, we lose contact with the very ground we are walking on.

As a driver in a car, when you look in the rear-view mirror, your focus naturally moves to the horizon and takes in the whole scene. Yet, when you look ahead through the windshield your vision naturally narrows to the road, the cars in your path, pedestrians or cyclists in the periphery and so on. If a driver were to look ahead at the holistic view while in busy traffic, they would be bound to get into an accident because their focus is required on certain specific variables in their environment.

Thus, the difference between the past and the future is that the past does not require our active participation in it, whereas the future does. Pre-emptively accepting whatever happens by default without discernment, preference or clear determination is a mechanism of avoidance. In treating the future as if it's already happened, we are trying to accept suffering before it happens in order to take the sting out of it.

---

36. https://www.nytimes.com/2018/07/11/nyregion/shambhala-sexual-misconduct.html
37. https://whatnow727.wordpress.com/2017/08/12/rigpa-announces-plans-for-independent-investigation-of-abuse-allegations/

The Trap

This is the dark side of spirituality and spiritual teachings. They provide a philosophical perspective from which to make sense of, and find acceptance for, the often-senseless things that happen to us. Yet, they do not balance this out with the practical wisdom that offers guidance on how to move forward and act decisively in a truthful, ethical and decisive manner. Instead, they promote a do-nothing, laissez-faire approach to living which generates its own brand of suffering. This is why it comes as no surprise that many seekers who eventually feel they have come to the realization of who they are still have no clue about what to do.

'There is nothing to do', 'There is no doer', 'Doership is an illusion' and other philosophical statements like these become toxic when they override our basic practical programs for day to day survival and interaction, because they turn us into flaccid and ineffectual creatures who can no longer tell up from down or right from wrong.

If an armed robber comes to my door and threatens to hurt my family, I will act in a manner to neutralize that individual at all costs. Does that mean I am incapable of seeing that this person themselves is a victim of social injustice? That through the process of harm, grief and loss my family too would evolve and learn much from the experience? That in the big picture whether a friend comes to my front door or an enemy, I will grow from both experiences regardless? Of course not. I am perfectly capable of seeing all that.

And yet, I am also capable of taking a baseball bat to the fucker's head, because that would be the need of the moment.

All the well-intentioned readers who are using their own experiences of learning from the good gurus and from the fake gurus too, and claiming that had it not been for both they would not have been who they are today, are right in saying so. Both *were* required. Yet, when they go on to say that we should not be overly critical of the culture, they are mistaken in saying so. Yes, we must absolutely be critical of a culture in which abuse, exploitation and neglect are systemic. Especially, when the number of critical voices, opposing the sheer volume of such teachers, are so few.

You have made the fundamental error of applying the lens of philosophical wisdom to the future. And in doing so you have fallen into the very trap these teachers and teachings have invented in order to keep their followers from mutinying against their masters.

The spiritual industry has done to seekers what consumerism has done to consumers: it has created the illusion of freedom, so no one ever has the motivation to revolt.

Paradoxical Wisdom

Paradoxical wisdom evolves and develops from experience and an unflinching resolve to face whatever life offers.

We do not have to dominate life like those of a more materialistic bent of mind. Nor do we claim to submit to life like those of a spiritual bent. We cooperate with it, we co-create with it. We are guided by it, yet we are equally willing to guide, should that be appropriate.

The self is not turned into some weapon of mass destruction as a result of alienating ourselves from life, nor is it converted into a limp dishrag by rationalizing our own will and volition into oblivion. We are an equal dance partner with the universe.

Which means that sometimes we are called on to follow and sometimes we are called on to lead. Sometimes we are called upon to accept what is happening around us and sometimes we are called on to resist. We hold both the holistic and dualistic views of life simultaneously in our view, with each giving context to the other.

We can act in a black and white manner even as we are seeing infinite shades of gray in front of us. Because that may be what the need of the moment is. We are not hampered from acting decisively by our holistic view of life. Nor are we prevented by our dualistic view from accepting our past as wholly beneficial to us.

We have a clear understanding that what we draw benefit from may not be apparently beneficial by nature.

Paradoxical wisdom is what brings the wisdom of being and the wisdom of doing into harmony, even though they appear to be in conflict on the surface.

It allows us to act in clear rebellion, even from a space of deep acceptance.

If that is the need of the hour.

Chapter 42
SPIRITUAL PYRAMID SCHEME

Q: I think the way you write about spirituality is down to earth and relatable in a way that anyone can see what you are talking about in their own experience. But, if I'm being honest, I do have a bone to pick with you. There is a part of me that goes, *Oh yeah, it's easy for you to have this clarity of perspective. You've had that awakening experience.* It's as if part of me needs that experience. I get what you are talking about intellectually. But it feels like if I haven't had it then I won't really be able to live life with the kind of understanding that you have.

A: Yes, I can appreciate where you're coming from. And all I can say is that you are greatly mistaken.

You don't need to have any such awakening experience to get clear on your own life. All you need is a real willingness, which is something that can't be forced. What you can do is rectify some of the misconceptions and hangups that are keeping you from developing that willingness. And that's what my writing on this page attempts to inspire people to do.

You have to understand that this whole enlightenment/awakening rhetoric is just a spiritual version of the get-rich-quick scheme.

Think about who the readers of those get-rich books are: they are usually people who are struggling financially in their own lives and have exhausted every avenue they can think of to try and generate a substantial income. Along comes a book by some billionaire who seems to have made his money by defying all the odds and rules that govern most of us. He promises that the secret to being like him is actually quite simple. Anyone can do it. Absolutely anyone can become a billionaire in a matter of a few years or even months if one applies the simple techniques he has outlined for them.

So, what do his readers do? They invest their hard-earned dollars in his books, merchandise, seminars, workshops and so on for years. Pretty soon those 'basic techniques' have turned into an obsession, at the end of which those readers will find themselves not a dollar richer for the time they've put in. Because there is one technique he left out of his books: the simplest and most obvious one staring everyone in the face. And that is—there is no such thing as simply getting rich. Everyone who gets rich does so at the expense of someone else. And the kicker is that you, his reader, are the 'someone else' he is getting rich off. He isn't reaching out to you so that he can uplift you. He is casting his line so he can reel you in.

The same is true of the spiritually impoverished: those consumed by their existential trials and tribulations who are seeking that one individual who has struck the spiritual goldmine of enlightenment. And that guru is going to do exactly what he needs to to reel you in and make you believe that you too can have what he has. You too can experience the kind of spiritual vision he does. You too can put an end to your suffering and finally enjoy the abundance and joy of what life has to offer. Who can resist such an offer?

So, you buy this guy's books, attend his retreats and satsangs, subscribe to his online channel and so on. And the more you hanker for what he has to offer the more he reels you in.

Whether you are chasing a get-rich scheme or an enlightenment scheme, the dynamics are essentially the same.

But take a moment to think for a second. What was this get-rich scheme really about for you before it became about getting rich? It was about wealth. And wealth is just another word for value. In other words, even though you may not be able to see it that way, what you are really in search of is learning how to perceive greater value in things. And that has unfortunately been translated by your mind as getting more dollars.

It's because you feel that your life is lacking in some way, that you think that it is the money that is lacking. Yet, what may be truly lacking here, even if financial hardship is the case, is your perspective. Because if you can't see the value in the 10 dollars you have to your name, there is no guaranteeing you will see the value in it even if that 10 dollars became 100 dollars, 1000 dollars or even a 1,000,000 dollars.

Wealth and abundance have little to do with one's circumstances. They are a mindset. It is possible to have only a few grand in the bank and feel rich. It is also possible to have hundreds of thousands and feel like one is scraping the bottom of the barrel. I know people like this.

The same is the case with awakening or enlightenment or whatever you want to call it. Take a moment to think about what getting enlightened really was about for you before it became about enlightenment. Before it became about oneness, transcendence, non-doership and all that nonsense. It was simply about wanting to know what the fuck was going on with you. Why the hell are you suffering so much? Why is it all so foggy and unclear?

In other words, you wanted to get clarity about yourself. It wasn't about transcendence or awakening or any of those things at first. You probably didn't even know what any of those words even meant. It was just this basic desire to see things more clearly.

Yet, your mind came in contact with spiritual teachings and culture and began to think that because it was lacking in clarity what it needed was something external, something extraordinary, to happen. Yet, here also what is lacking is not your experience, mystical or otherwise. It is your perspective that is lacking. Because if you can't see the value in the awareness you have today, no matter how limited, there is no guaranteeing you will see the value in the awareness you have after one, ten or even a hundred awakening experiences.

Clarity does not result from accumulating spiritual or mystical revelations. Clarity is the direct result of a mindset that is open and inquisitive. It is quite possible to have had zero spiritual revelations or earth-shattering insights and develop a crystal clarity about oneself. It is equally possible to have had staggering *satoris* and still be totally delusional.

On these pages, I have been open about my own awakening experience because I have no reason to pretend like it didn't happen. At the same time, I have never held it as some badge of achievement because I simply don't see it as one. Hitting the jackpot at the slot machine may make you temporarily rich but it sure as hell isn't going to teach you the value of money. Similarly, awakening is a spiritually enriching experience but it does not, in the long run, reveal anything of how to live a life of value.

Only clarity can do that. And clarity *never* comes all at once. It is an ever refining process.

So (if you can bear with me stretching this analogy just a bit further), rather than telling people how to 'get rich', what is essential is showing people how to understand the value of the wealth one already possesses. The experience of being 'rich' lies more in your perspective than it does in your circumstances. *How* you value what you have is several orders of magnitude more essential than what you have.

The same is true of clarity and understanding. And that is what I write about. Forget about any kinds of experience others are having that you could also have. Start with reality exactly the way it appears for you. That is all you will ever need. Everything that you are in search of is laid out in front of you plain as the light of day, right under your nose. You just can't see it because you haven't learned how to value reality. You feel that reality, the truth, needs to be something more: more profound, more spiritual, more liberating.

But I can guarantee you no matter how many profound, spiritual or liberating experiences you have, you will be no closer to seeing yourself and your circumstances with any greater clarity.

Because the very mechanism that keeps you seeking is what prevents you from seeing. It is what prevents you from being open to life as it is happening because you are focused on life as you think it should happen.

As I mentioned in the beginning, all we need is a real willingness to look. And that willingness only emerges when every pyramid scheme with which our minds are infatuated reveals itself as the hollow enterprise it really is.

Chapter 43

BOMBS AWAY!

Let me set the record straight, because you may be confused as to what I am about.

I'm not here to prove anything to you. I'm not here to be liked or validated by you. And I'm certainly not here to convince you to be anything like me. You couldn't even if you tried. Your best case scenario, in this life, is if you ended up being something like yourself.

I'm also not here to claim anything. What's there to claim? I have a body. So do you. I have a brain. So, do you. I have a penis. Half of you do. And the other half are lucky to have dodged *that* bullet. I get hungry when I haven't eaten. I get cranky when I haven't slept. I get frustrated when things don't work out for me. I feel good when things do.

No surprises there. What's there to claim?

Anything else I say is just a perspective. A perspective on reality, a perspective on myself. I can share my perspective with you. But you can never share my perspective. All you can do is share your own. It's all just food for thought, nothing more. Take what I say with a grain of salt. If it's edible to you then welcome to this buffet. If it's not, there's plenty of other places you can find a meal. Or better yet, just learn to cook for yourself and you'll never go hungry again.

But whatever nonsense it is that you want to project on me is your own business.

If you're looking for perfection, you sure as hell ain't gonna find it here. So, let me save you a lot of disappointment.

'Shiv, are you enlightened?' No, there is no such thing.

'Shiv, are you 100% truthful?' No, there is no such thing.

'Shiv, are you happy all the time?' No, there is no such thing.

'Shiv, have you attained permanent inner peace?' No, there is no such thing.

'Shiv, are you motivated by a need to enlighten others?' No, I'm motivated by a need to do what I need to do in order to make this experience of life worthwhile for me.

'Shiv, are you motivated by a need to help others?' No, others need to take accountability for their own issues and help themselves. Not my business.

'Shiv, then why the hell am I listening to anything you have to say?' I honestly have no fucking idea. But just maybe, you want to listen to an average schmuck own his mediocre existence without apology.

Because make no mistake. I am mediocre. Better at some things than I am at others. But the net effect is that I am not worth emulating in the least.

I wear my mediocrity like a fucking badge. I'm happy to give 75% effort in all that I do and spend 25% of the time slacking off. I have volumes of unrealized potential within me that I have no intention of ever realizing. I can imagine no greater form of anxiety than having to fulfill my 'passionate purpose' day in and day out and give it my 100%.

Fuck. That. Shit.

I have no insider's information on the answers of the universe. I can barely remember what I ate for breakfast this morning. I have no special knowledge. I barely know ten percent of what is already out there as proven scientific fact. I am *not* an intellectual by any means. Put me in a room full of them and this will become rapidly apparent.

I'm just a guy using his limited brain and common sense to reflect on his own conscious experience and reporting what he has seen and understood as a result of that reflection. It's quite possible that I am completely delusional. There is no way for you to really know that. All you can do is compare your own perspective with mine and perform a gap analysis in order to determine how out of sync the two are. The closer they align, the more on the level I will seem. The more out of phase they are, the more delusional I will sound to you.

I don't give two fornications.

The only reason you should want to emulate me is if you're the world's biggest loser and can't even aspire to your own mediocrity. But other than that, you're better off looking for other role models.

Still, don't despair. You won't have to look far. A whole list of experts will appear with an antidote to every one of your woes. They'll teach you to heal, to excel, to elevate, to actualize. All kinds of cool solutions to elevate you from your own average existence into the:

BEST
COOLEST
MOST LOVING
MOST ENLIGHTENED

Version of **you**rself

Not here. Here you get your own shitty mediocrity rubbed in your face and mirrored back to you *ad nauseam*.

But hey, some people like that. Some people have a fetish for ordinary things. Some people have a hard on for the mundane. Folks be kinky like that. Don't judge, you prude!

Some people don't want to reach some higher place of consciousness, transcend their own suffering, realize their most passionate purpose, break the wheel of samsara or even solve the world's crises. None of those awesome prizes other contestants in the game of life seem to be gunning for.

Some people are just sitting here going: 'So, let's see. I have another ten, twenty, thirty, forty odd years on this planet? Okay, I can either waste my time moaning about my lot. Or I could just enjoy whatever the hell this is until the party's over.'

Let the next fucking incarnation deal with getting me off the *wheel of samsara*! I've got no time for that shit.

Did I mention procrastination? There's something I absolutely excel at.

This isn't about 'enlightenment'. It's about lightening up. If 7.8 billion people, in this very moment, stopped taking themselves so fucking seriously, a lot of things would change very fast.

But that's not going to happen and that's okay because that's really none of my business either. The only business I have, that I am responsible for, is making it through this lifetime without totally fucking things up.

And this is easier said than done, because we are hardcoded to fuck things up. Which is why old Buddha talked about sticking to the middle path. Be average! Be mediocre! That way at least when you do fuck up, it'll just be an average kind of mess you create. And with a mediocre effort, you'll learn to clean it up.

Not enlightenment. But entitlement. That's our problem.

Actually believing, that *me: my* problems, *my* suffering, *my* passion, *my* realization, *my* actualization is what any of this is about.

The other day I got a flat tire and, as I sweated and swore while changing it, a passing crow took a shit on my shoulder. That is how much sympathy life actually has for what any of us are going through.

And I looked at that steaming bird-dropping and laughed. Because I had, in my frustration and irritation at the flat tire, actually for a moment believed that I was some special entity who didn't deserve such things to happen to him. I had taken my own existence seriously enough to feel a sense of injustice about a flat tire.

Take that!

The moment the shit bomb hit my shoulder, the feeling of injustice turned into a mushroom cloud of hopeless despair for a split instant, before the sheer absurdity of it all freed me from my own sense of self-importance. Laughter was all there was left.

As long as I am the joke, there's an endless supply of laughs to be had...

So, lighten up a little. I'm not some enlightened dude here to teach you to liberate yourself.

Best-case scenario: I'm just a crow taking a shit on your shoulder.

Chapter 44

BREAK ON THROUGH

Q: I am unable to see much of a point in life. It's like that Louis C.K. standup where he wonders why more people don't just kill themselves. Why don't they? Not that I want to. I'm too chicken and too worried about what that would do to people who love me. But intellectually it feels like a logical choice. Everything feels hollow. I've become a nihilist. I feel like a lost cause. A loser. Why am I so cynical? I want to go back to being ignorant again. Ignorance really is bliss. I feel I'm being too cynical...

A: And I feel you're not being cynical enough.

What is cynicism? It is an attitude of mistrust—of authority figures, of social mores, of institutions, of belief systems, of social dynamics, of rules of engagement, of political ideologies, of spiritual doctrine... it is to suspect that the very scaffolding upon which all of what we see has been built, is a sham. And when we begin to see this, often against our own will and volition, we have no choice but to feel jaded by the whole experience.

There is a bitterness and a resentment that brews inside. There is a feeling of having been duped by this elaborate scheme that everyone has been a part of. There is the disappointment in realizing that even those we believed were wise like our parents, our teachers, our gurus, our leaders were just fools like the rest of them. Everyone fell for it.

If you've ever been conned, you know that it doesn't feel good.

To rub salt into the wound, it's not like you can just walk

away from it all either. Sure you could go hide in a cave or a forest somewhere. But if that's not your cup of tea, then you are pretty much stuck living in the sham. Every news report, every TV ad, every celebrity performance, every spiritual satsang, even ordinary social interactions like small talk by the office cooler, or getting chatted up at someone's party is a grating feeling on your senses. It all reeks of hypocrisy, idiocy, confusion, falsehood.

Why would you want to be in the world when that world is a cesspool of lies, fabrication, pretentiousness, fear, insecurity, manipulation and exploitation?

You are right to say that the world is empty and devoid of real meaning. It is hollow to the core.

But that world is not life. It's a tiny aspect of it. The human drama. With its elaborate sets and elaborate scripts and elaborate roles and elaborate costumes. It's like stumbling into a Hollywood set, except this set encompasses most of the globe.

Not cynical enough...

Because you still think of yourself as a 'lost cause' or 'a loser'. Compared to what? Compared to whom?

What is a loser? What is a winner? You can only have losers if you also have winners. So, what are we talking about winning and losing at? Life? Everyone loses in life. Reaching the finish line earns you the prize of a wooden box six feet under the ground or a bed of sticks set ablaze.

Winning and losing is about the human drama for you. And if you feel like a loser then there is something within you that *still* believes you can win.

Not cynical enough. Not skeptical enough. Not nihilistic enough.

You've whittled away many of your beliefs but there are some fundamental ones still lurking just beneath the surface that are totally fucking with your mind.

When in doubt, double down. That's been my motto ever

since I began to see through the facade. The moment I begin to feel an inner wavering, an inner questioning of my own self in relation to my environment, an inner hesitation to act in a manner that feels true to me for fear of how it may be perceived, I override my instinct to brake by hitting the gas pedal instead.

Trust your cynicism. The energy of it. Not the content of it. Not what it's saying to you. But where it's taking you.

You can't discover life's meaning until you have drowned in its total meaninglessness. You can't affirm life until you have utterly denied it. You can't discover your reason to live until you have exhausted all the reasons why you shouldn't.

Anything short of that is a decoy. It's a substitute. An impostor ideal handed to you by someone or something outside of you. They are not *your* reasons.

Anarchy is the highest form of governance. But the world isn't ready for it. We still need to be led, to be policed, to be told right from wrong, to be judged, to be worked, to be told how much we owe, to be held responsible for our actions, to be rewarded for our good deeds and punished for our bad ones—like children. Like witless children.

But the chick that grows too large for its shell begins to feel constricted by it. The chick feels the pressure and stress of a world that it has outgrown. And it pecks. It pecks like mad, in a frenzy, in desperation to break free—to get out of this structure that once nourished the chick, but is now slowly crushing it.

Keep pecking.

There is a bigger reality out there that has little to do with what human beings think or say about it. You can't see it because this shell is all you know. This shell of ideology, identity, ideas, idiocy.

And it may seem like you have a death wish. To the chick who is compelled to destroy its shell, it may seem like an act of self-sabotage; of annihilation of its world and thereby its self. But what the chick doesn't realize is that it is really obeying its own impulse to live. To encounter life raw and real. To be separated no longer by an opaque wall that keeps the chick cocooned in a world of warm isolation.

Life, raw and unfiltered, is rife with meaning. Not the kind of 'meaning' the intellect craves. But the kind that is self-evident, self-explanatory, self-justifying in the absolute immediacy with which the moment appears.

Follow your discontent. Follow your disgust. Follow your mistrust and your cynicism. Follow it until you are standing outside that shell of your former self.

From that vantage point things are seen differently. The human stage becomes no more than a form of entertainment. Our plots and storylines no more than substandard and hackneyed scripts. Our roles and identities no more than over-the-top caricatures of ourselves.

And instead of a guttural moan of dismay, all this absurdity evokes is a great and unrestrained belly laugh.

Chapter 45

I AM NOT, YET I AM

'I am not the thinker of my thoughts'.
'I am not the doer of my deeds.'
'There is no one here that is witnessing this.'
'Thinking, doing, witnessing happens without cause.'

These were the words that came out of my mouth when I experienced my first awakening.

It was a staggering realization to see everything as one great movement. The universe still in the midst of that first bang. All the words, the thoughts, the actions, the desires that I had believed were my own and chosen by me—just part and parcel of that singular bang—still happening, happening, forever happening.

No I nor you. No this nor that. No here nor there. No now nor then. No cause nor effect. All just an endless unfolding and unpacking of a singular explosive event.

Space, time, matter, energy, self, world: these bedrock constants upon which our realities are based suddenly appeared completely fluid, elastic, changeable, hollow.

The world began to appear increasingly surreal—dreamlike. Everything, including nature, began to appear artificial—as if it were all made of plastic. My body too felt like something artificial, plastic, manufactured off some faceless assembly line.

My mind began to feel similarly artificial. Like an AI programmed with myriad algorithms. My thoughts, my ideas, my opinions—nothing felt original to me. They felt like implants. Furthermore, I had no control over when the thoughts occurred, how they took hold of me, what they convinced me to do, what other thoughts or emotional experiences or actions they triggered. It all seemed like an elaborate game my mind was playing with itself as I just sat uselessly watching and being moved like a puppet. Even the 'watching' seemed to happen beyond me and my control.

'Then where the fuck am I?' I couldn't find myself! There simply was no 'I' in this equation that was in any way separate from what was occurring. Any 'sense' of a self that there was, was only another appearance like space or time or matter.

At first, all of this felt immensely liberating, because it freed me of the burden that my own identity had become. I had suffered so intensely, hated my self so much, wished it destroyed, been ashamed of it, felt tormented by it. Imagine being the captive of some abusive kidnapper and suffering as their hostage for years. And then one day you realize the kidnapper is no longer there. They've just vanished.

Seeing that the story of my self was not only a piece of fiction, but also that the self was a mirage created by a trick of the mind, like seeing a face in the clouds, was like being set free from my captor.

I believed I was enlightened. In fact, I had no doubt about it.

Yet, I struggled to orient myself to this new reality. I had lost my bearings on reality altogether.

What was good, what was bad? What was right or wrong? Where was up or down? What was now, what was later? I became dysfunctional to a large extent. I had lost my coordinates and was drifting listlessly on an empty ocean of nonsensical experience that had no end.

I couldn't relate to people easily because I had no language by which to relate. I didn't understand rules of speech, decorum, boundaries of appropriateness. Everything became open season. Morality, ethics, laws, empathy, decency—none of these held much meaning.

Why can't I eat rotten food? What's the point of eating at all? Why can't one sleep with another man's wife? Why can't one sleep with another man's pet? Why can't we just cannibalize each other for food? Why can't I just step off the second storey balcony and see if my kneecaps shatter on impact, just for the heck of it?

What at first seemed like great freedom and sanity soon devolved into a madness that I wouldn't wish upon anyone. When it's all uncaused, when there is no 'thinker' to the thoughts, when there is no 'doer' to the deeds—there also ceases to be a 'regulator' of what is thought, said and done. The conscience is annihilated.

Yet, even in the absence of a separate self, the mind was still pumping out thoughts and emotions by the second. And this emotional roller coaster became terrifying at one point. The highs were intense highs and the lows were devastating lows. I lived in pure survival mode. Through it all, I struggled to function in my daily life: hold a job, pay rent, feed myself.

It's all made up. It's all arbitrary. There is no real north or south, east or west. There is only this endless ocean of experience!

At a certain point I came to realize that this was an unfeasible way to live. I had entered a realm of pure chaos. And if a life had to be lived, it needed an anchor around which perception could be ordered and life could be structured.

That anchor was the self.

Whether the self was real or illusory wasn't the point. The point was that just like my 'sense' of hearing converted waves of energy into sound, just like my 'sense' of sight converted waves of energy into shapes and colors, just like my 'sense' of touch converted waves of energy into solid, liquid or vapor—so also did my 'sense' of self convert waves of energy and information, coming from my nervous system, into *me*.

'I am as real as the redness of a rose. I am as real as the resonance of a guitar string. I am as real as the hardness of this table. I am of the same nature as all that I see, feel, touch, smell and hear.

'If I am an illusion, then this is all an illusion too. So, we are of the same nature regardless. Then what is "real" and what is "illusory"? Only words.

'Reality. Illusion. Are they separate? Are they not two aspects of the same?

'One may say the rose is real. Redness is only an illusion. But a rose without redness isn't a rose. And redness cannot exist without a form like the rose to manifest it.

'A rose without "redness" is simply an idea of a rose. A table without "hardness" is simply an idea of a table. A guitar string without its resonance is simply the idea of a guitar string. This world, without me, is simply the idea of a world.

'I am the essence of what it means for something to "exist". I am what gives reality its "realness". I am not real. I am realness itself.'

As my self reassumed its former position: mountains once again became mountains. Rivers once again became rivers.

In a world innately free of coordinates, it became my responsibility to set my own coordinates. In the absence of any real cardinal directions, I established my own north and south using the magnetic pull of my intuition. I used my wife, my first daughter and then my second daughter as my three anchors to reality. And the deep love I felt for them became the immovable weight that held those anchors firm. I began building a new scaffolding around my life. A new set of rules by which to play the game...

Realizing that it's all a made-up game is one thing. Yet, as revelatory as that is, sitting on the bench for the rest of the game just because 'it's all made up' is a waste of a lifetime. Much better not to realize anything, if that's the case! But getting off the bench and rejoining the game, knowing full well it's a game, is where true freedom lies. And that is also where true responsibility lies, because now you are not only responsible for how you play but also responsible for the game itself.

'I am not the thinker of my thoughts. Yet, I choose to be.'

'I am not the doer of my deeds. Yet, I choose to be.'

'There is no one here that is witnessing this. Yet, I choose to be.'

'Thinking, doing, witnessing happen without cause. Yet, I choose to be the cause of it all.'

Chapter 46

HALO OF HOPE

Q: The thing for me is an almost depressive meaninglessness when it becomes clear that what I have done all my life, trying to get somewhere else and find what I'm looking for, didn't work. But I gave all my identity in that and all the purpose of life. So now what? I can understand what you mean with the simplicity and the play and wonder of how it all is, but I feel that my motivation is damaged and very low!

A: Seeing fully into the futility of all these searches we embark upon to 'find' ourselves, our truth, our purpose, our happiness, this *has* to be depressing.

Finally realizing that there is absolutely no chance or route of escape *has* to be deflating.

Grasping that no matter what you do, achieve, understand or create you will not have improved upon this moment as it already stands even an iota, one *has* to be inundated by a sense of meaninglessness.

Fully comprehending that evolution is ultimately a circular movement around an unchanging core of experience, one *has* to be drained of purpose and motivation.

Let me assure you that what you are experiencing is not outside the norm. It *is* the norm. Getting sober is a tremendously deflating experience.

The truth is you haven't really been drained of purpose, meaning, motivation and such. You have been denied the substance that had hijacked all those things from you and was only giving it to you on its *own* terms. That substance is the future.

The future has always been your escape route. And the future has hijacked your sense of self, your purpose, your meaning and motivation. It has captivated them and made you believe that, since it holds the things you value the most, then *it* must be more valuable than the present.

It has created a decoy. A copycat identity. A perfect replica of yourself—except for certain cosmetic modifications. Your future self is the photoshopped version of you—minus many of the flaws and blemishes you sport while highlighting your assets. Most importantly, it has enveloped your image in a halo of 'hope'. Because that is what the true enchantment of the future is. That is its spell. That is the advantage it holds over the present. And so, the present self can never compete with the future self, because it will always lack that halo.

The future hijacked you a long time ago just as it did me and billions of others. And most people will languish and eventually die never knowing how they were bewitched by it their entire lives.

Yet, something caused you to snap out of it and come to your senses. You've begun to see the dead end in this 'escape route' of the future. Something in you senses that that isn't your home, it isn't where you belong. Home is here and now. Except…

'I knew who I was in the future. *But who am I, here?'*

'I knew what purpose the future held for me because of all the plans I created. *But what purpose do I have, now?'*

'I knew how the future motivated me to act through its various goals and milestones. *But how will the present motivate me?'*

'I knew the meaning my life had through the various dreams and hopes I held. *But with what ingredients am I to create meaning in this moment, when it is devoid of dreams and hope?'*

The present feels like returning home to a land you left when you were still a child and have lived away from for a lifetime. What you are experiencing is a reverse culture shock. A reorientation that begins with disorientation.

You cannot rediscover meaning without going through a phase of meaninglessness. You cannot rediscover purpose without going through a phase of purposelessness. You cannot rediscover your self without going through a phase of not knowing who or what you are.

That limbo is where you are. But that limbo needn't be purgatory. It's just a matter of developing the right perspective around what is happening.

The halo is missing. That hope that filled in all those empty spaces, that smoothed over all the rough edges, that reconciled all the seeming gaps, that repaired all the broken bridges. The reality of the present isn't so neat, isn't so clear cut: it is full of paradoxes and riddles, missing pieces and puzzling occurrences. And the self we encounter in the present is equally paradoxical—with glaring blemishes that can't just be smoothed away, gaps and spaces which can't just be colored in.

Yet, the present has one thing the future doesn't have. And that is 'depth'. No matter what, the future only exists in 2D. You can photoshop the image all you want but you can never bring it to life. You can never see all its dimensions at once. All you have to work with is a two-dimensional replica of the real deal.

Within every human being is a tug-of-war between truth and hope. Between being and becoming. Between what-is and what-could-be. And when the pull of truth within us overwhelms the pull of hope, we find ourselves with our feet firmly planted in the present.

You have resigned yourself to the present but have yet to fully accept it.

Acceptance is not resignation.

Even though you have placed yourself in the present you are still thinking in the language of the future. That is why the meaning, the purpose, the motivation still eludes you. You have lived abroad so long you have forgotten your native tongue and are only able to think in a foreign language.

Give it time.

If the future has truly lost its hold on you, your mind will reorient to its new circumstances. It will learn the language of the present. It will reclaim its meaning and its purpose and assert it in this new territory. But it will do so in a new way. In a way that you can't quite envision as yet, because you are still accustomed to thinking of yourself as a future-based entity.

When the halo of hope has lost its shine, when the fire of hell has lost its heat, then you will find yourself no longer drawn to saints nor terrified by demons.

Instead, with your feet planted in the cool mud of truth, you will discover a whole different way of being. You will learn about purpose from the trees, about meaning from the passing clouds, about motivation from the birds and the ants who ceaselessly build their lives one present moment at a time.

Chapter 47

TO WAKE OR NOT TO WAKE

Q: There's nothing to achieve. This is it. What's the point of talking about any of this? Why are we so interested in 'awakening'? Why is it so important? Why do teachers talk about awakening like it's the most incredibly important experience on the planet? Why can't I just go back to the story of me? Why not take the blue pill and continue living in the Matrix?

A: Why not? That's a perfectly reasonable choice to make.

Awakening isn't important. It isn't even necessary. What you realize or fail to realize makes not an ounce of difference to the overall scheme of things.

I know most of the stuff you've heard directly contradicts what I am saying. To awaken to your own true nature has been marketed to you as the highest virtue a being can aspire to. It is 'breaking the karmic cycle'. It is 'getting off the wheel of birth and rebirth'. It is having 'compassion for all sentient beings'. It is seeing, like the Buddha did, that 'all beings are enlightened'. It is breaking the chains of suffering and becoming liberated once and for all.

Except...

... It's still all about *you*. And life simply couldn't care what you do or don't do, what you see or don't see, what you realize or don't realize. Even other people don't really care that much. If they appear to care it's because they really care about themselves and wish the same for themselves. The only person who this is actually important to—is you.

Awakening, self-realization and most things spiritual are only new stories we tell ourselves when the old stories we were living out begin to seem boring and predictable. That's not to say such experiences don't exist. Certainly they do. Awakening is an experience as real as my sitting here and typing this sentence.

But is it important? Is it essential? Is it the highest virtue you can aspire to?

How you answer that depends on the lens through which the question is being asked.

If the lens is a self-centric one, if it's a worldview where your self is the centre around which the universe has been constructed and its values prioritized? Then, *Yes!* Awakening *is* important, essential and the highest virtue.

In such a self-centric view, what greater importance could there be than to liberate the very core around which the entire universe revolves and upon which all of reality hinges? Awakening is the pinnacle of all experiences! To be enlightened thus, is to enlighten all beings. Because when the root is awakened the whole tree that emerges from it must spring to life! You *are* that root. There can be no greater act of virtue than this. What human endeavor could be more essential? To say that awakening is 'important' is the greatest understatement of all time.

With the self at the centre, the fate of the universe literally depends upon you. What choice will you make? Will you choose just another mundane sheep-like existence: being fed your views, your beliefs, your ideas and your stories of self? Or will you choose the extraordinary path of realization and casting aside all falsehoods one by one in an effort to reveal the truth? Which movie will you star in? Will it be a dull and forgettable TV drama? Or a ground-breaking, award-winning, box-office record-setting, blockbuster of the year?

As the hero of your own narrative, what could be more important than to undertake a 'hero's journey'? From rags to riches. From disillusionment to triumph. From suffering to liberation.

That moment when you finally awaken and proclaim as the Buddha did, 'All beings are enlightened.'

Do you hear that?

That's the sound of the whole universe applauding!

Or...

...There is the lens through which no such self sits at the centre of it all. The self is just a passing phenomenon like a cloud formation in the sky. In such a view, there is no center to the universe. All points are equally valid. Everything affects everything else. Nothing remains for long. Even the brightest supernovas and the densest black holes are passing phenomena that have a momentary effect and then are totally forgotten.

In this view, what happens or doesn't happen for a single particular self is of minimal consequence. Whether you awaken or don't. Whether you realize something of yourself or don't is of very little significance. Whether you burst into a blaze of illumination like a supernova or collapse into a dense void like a black hole is of negligible importance. The universe has seen many like you and will encounter many more to come.

From the viewpoint of the whole, no point within it is more or less significant than another. No phenomenon happening within it is more or less significant. The joyous shout of a Buddha as he proclaims his enlightenment and the spurious moans of a sex-worker in a fake climax are of equal significance. A sage waking up to the reality of his true nature and a teenager waking up to the reality of another school day are both utterly ordinary phenomena.

All are ordinary. Nothing is extraordinary. For if something were to be extraordinary, something else would have to be less-than-ordinary. And to the whole, nothing can be more or less than whole. Everything is of the same nature as itself.

From this lens of perception, the answer to your questions

is a resounding *No*! Your awakening is not essential. Not important. Not the highest virtue a human can aspire to. It is just another mundane event in the universe: like a cloud dissipating.

The great irony, then, is that 'awakening' is simply a shift in perspective from the first lens to the second.

It is a reordering of one's worldview from self-centric to centerless. And in the process, all those events of spiritual significance, all the revelations we crave and value, all our hopes and aspirations are razed back to the ground level at which all phenomena exist. Everything becomes absolutely ordinary and of no special significance—including awakening.

If our spiritual teachers were really awakened they would be telling us this. They would be like dull and humorless parents, dousing the fires of our romantic spiritual views with their sobering perspectives rather than fanning the flames for their own amusement or benefit.

Like teenage girls or boys who believe that finding their perfect soulmate is the purpose of their life, spiritual seekers are driven by hopelessly romantic ideas of enlightenment. A good parent is one who neither discourages nor encourages the teenager, yet simply adds a sober perspective that the teen may not fully comprehend as yet, but which will in time make greater sense. Similarly, a teacher, if they are truly wise, will neither egg on the seeker, nor will they command them to cease and desist. They will simply present a sober perspective that says:

None of this is really as significant as you are making it out to be.

The seeker may not fully comprehend this, but in time it will make greater sense.

Of course, what most teachers actually do is egg on their students. They are like parents who claim, *I have found my own soulmate and you will too one day if you just believe!* They rarely question the fundamental premise of lack that is driving the seeker's seeking. And they hardly ever talk of awakening as the ordinary experience that it is.

Seeking, finding, awakening, realizing. None of this is of any real significance.

If given the choice to live another lifetime under an entirely different storyline—I would gladly choose something completely different. Rather than the theme of spiritual realization, I'd pick another genre entirely. Perhaps, a life of crime or being a member of an undiscovered Amazonian tribe. So many genres of fiction to pick from. The only reason we pigeonhole ourselves in our narratives is because we actually believe that a genre such as 'non-fiction' exists. Spirituality is not non-fiction. It's just another genre like the rest.

So, why not take the blue pill and live in the Matrix? Or take the red pill and step out of the Matrix. It's all just as well. Both choices are equally valid. Neither is of greater significance than the other. Neither of higher virtue. Neither is going to save you from the death that is imminent. The universe isn't going to give much of a shit. You won't get an applause. You may receive a scattered clapping from a few people around the world who are obsessed with the same things you are. But they are really clapping for themselves, not for you.

For me, the question of which pill to take is inconsequential. It makes no difference whether I place my self in the Matrix or apart from it. Blue or red? It's as significant as asking me what my favorite color is. It's only a matter of preference and nothing more.

Because what I see through my own lens is that I *am* the Matrix.

Chapter 48
THERE IS NO HOW

Q: I've tried looking at the fucking tree, man. I don't know what I'm doing wrong. You say 'Truth is evident' but I don't know how to see it. How do I see it? This stuff has been driving me crazy for years. I'm so fed up. Just wanna be done with it. How to be free? How to be happy? How to be at peace? How to let go?

A: The boy is on the beach busy building a sandcastle. And each time the wave comes in and wrecks his castle, he moans in despair and blames the universe for his woes. Yet, in the next moment, as he begins rebuilding, he is filled with positive emotion and hope when his castle begins taking shape again. Eventually, another big wave comes in and wrecks the castle and the boy cries out in dismay, lamenting that life as he knows it has lost all purpose...

You are being a child. Why do you think this 'stuff' has been driving you crazy all these years? Because what you've been indulging in is literally insane. You are attempting to find the 'one shape' of a castle that will withstand the big wave. There is no such shape. The big wave will destroy whatever you build no matter how sophisticated.

All these *how* questions you are asking: how to be happy, how to be free, how to see the truth, how to let go—what you are really asking me is: 'How do I build a castle that won't crumble?'

You can't. You won't. Castles are meant to crumble.

Can you imagine the boy who keeps rebuilding again and again in the desperate belief that he will hit that magic configuration one day? This is your problem. This is the source of your neurosis. You think 'truth' is some ideal or superior architecture that needs to be found through diligence and practice and perseverance.

That's why you've followed these teachers and gurus for so many years. These 'castle experts' who have just the right technique, the right practice, the right teaching that will provide a solution to all your problems. Do this meditation, inquire in this way, eat this, sit like this, sleep like this, fuck like this. They've got you jumping through hoops like a circus pony because that's how gullible you are.

You say you're fed up. You say you want to be done with it. Then, *Be Done With It!*

What's your excuse?

Sitting here asking another human being, *How do I do this? How do I do that?* is not going to get you anywhere. It keeps you stunted and child-like (and not in a good way). Only children ask their parents how they must do things because they are helpless. At least they have a good reason—they've only been alive for a handful of years. What's your excuse?

Your problem is not truth, happiness, peace or any of that. That is how you have *framed* the problem in your own mind because you want to avoid seeing the real problem.

And the real problem is that life isn't easy.

It holds an inherent dichotomy that makes us uncomfortable. Every moment of pleasure contains within it the seed of pain just waiting to sprout. Every new birth already prophesises a future death. Every good thing that happens to you is eventually going to go away. Everyone you love is eventually going to die in front of your very eyes, or you in front of theirs.

Every fragrant flower eventually rots and gives off a stench. Every innocent child eventually grows into a confused adult.

Even great marriages end in messy divorces. Even children who have been given everything by their parents grow up to forget all about what their parents did for them. No matter how much money you earn, no matter how much power you wield, no matter how much fame or influence you have, the burden of what you don't have will always outweigh the weight of what you do have.

Every single person alive on this planet today will be dead in another hundred years. And in time they will be entirely forgotten. Your life, your name, your entire existence will be like it never even happened.

Your entire lifetime will vanish like a self-deleting social media conversation.

That is what you simply cannot bear.

And you want it to be different. So you invent this alternate reality called 'enlightenment' where life *is* easy. And there are no problems in enlightenment-land. There is no happiness or sadness—only happiness. No peace or conflict—only peace. No truth or falsehood—only truth. *Sat, Chit, Ananda.*[38]

In other words, all you have done is taken the religious notion of Paradise and turned it into a place in the mind versus a place in the sky.

Earth is too painful and you want heaven. Isn't that what 'transcendence', 'ascending', 'higher self', 'higher consciousness' are all about? Look at the imagery and symbolism hidden in the words! It's all about *Going Up*. Up where? Up to what?

You've tried escaping in the horizontal direction—through work, relationships, alcohol, money—and none of that worked out for you. So now you just shifted your strategy to a vertical direction. Now, you are trying to escape upwards rather than sideways! That's all spirituality is—a vertical escape hatch.

People think Zazen is meditation. It is not. If there were a practice I would endorse as even remotely beneficial it is Zazen.

38. Truth, Consciousness, Bliss. A name for the unchanging reality.

And not the version it has become, with its bullshit rituals and gasshos[39] and other such nonsense.

All zazen is about is just sitting. Not meditating, not trying to experience insight, not trying to see reality, not trying to witness your own thoughts, not trying to be aware of awareness or some such pretentious crap. But literally… just sitting.

Because these Zen dudes realized that people like you are literally in escape mode twenty-four-fucking-seven. If there is an outlet to escape, you will take it. It could be a door, a window, a sewer, a ventilation shaft. Anything to get the fuck away from where you are right now.

So, the *only* solution they saw to this problem of compulsive escape was to sit put. If you were to translate the word 'Zazen' into its literal meaning in the context of when it was created, it would translate to 'just sit yer ass down!'

Forget heaven. Down to earth. Forget enlightenment. Back to basics.

That is what I subjected myself to for over a year. Hours and hours of just sitting on my balcony with nothing to do. Not meditating, not witnessing. Just using every ounce of self-control I had to prevent myself from leaping out of my own skin or jumping over the balcony. And it was through utter boredom and helplessness, seeing how deep that resistance was within me, that I came to realize what my real problem was.

It wasn't that I wasn't happy or at peace or whatever. It was that I couldn't bear discomfort. And the more I focused on the discomfort the more uncomfortable it felt—just like an itch that you can't reach. Sitting in self-imposed solitary confinement did two things. First, it developed courage within me to sit with the discomfort and take responsibility for it. Second, it allowed me to see how I was exponentially magnifying the discomfort by giving it undue significance.

All my existential angst was no more significant than an

39. Gassho: ritual Japanese hand gesture.

annoying itch. How many people are willing to look at their own suffering in such a mundane way? Imagine glorifying a skin rash into the greatest existential crisis to plague humanity! That is what we do with our suffering.

Truth *is* evident when you aren't desperately trying to look away from it.

Nobody told the boy that he has to build a castle. He sees other kids doing it so feels he should do so too. But neither the ocean nor the beach exist for the purpose of his castle. And when he is done sulking, he will realize it isn't all about him.

The real miracle here is that he has been given the opportunity to play. The beach provides the sand for him to create shapes with. The ocean provides the moisture with which the sand may hold together. This simple dynamic of interaction between water and sand allows him hours of endless play.

What a fucking miracle. Because if this were just a desert, the sand would be too dry to hold together. And if this were the ocean floor, there would be too much water for the sand to take shape. It is precisely the point where surf meets sand, that sandcastles are possible. And it's precisely here that the big wave will come in to eventually tear them down.

Truth is seeing this dynamic for what it is.

Happiness is enjoying the miraculous opportunity to play.

Peace is realizing that no matter what you build it will eventually be taken down and returned to its original form.

The system is flawless to begin with and nothing you can do can either improve or fuck it up.

So play. Just play.

When it comes to playing, there is no *how.*

Chapter 49

I DO NOT KNOW

Q: For someone who claims not to have answers, you appear to know a lot! I don't mean that as a criticism, btw. If you really don't know, why have you written so many articles?

A: I don't know anything. Not with any certainty. Not about the absolute nature of reality.

All I have are my own personal experiences to go by. As to everything else extrapolated from there, it is a working hypothesis. Nothing more.

Everything I know, everything I understand, is relative. It's in relation to, or in negation of, some other form of knowledge or understanding out there. I know nothing about what reality is. All I can talk about is what it isn't.

So my knowledge, my words, my articles are mostly relative. They are not designed to tell you what life is. Only to say what it isn't. They are designed to dismantle already held and cherished views about what reality is. And to reorient the attention away from the mind's desperate desire to grasp what this is. Because to grasp it is to lose it.

Everything I know is only relative to what *you* know. I use my knowledge as a weapon to disarm you. But my weapon cannot create anything. It cannot illuminate. All it can do is cut down.

Like a machete that clears out an opening in an overgrown forest, my words can only open up a space, an opportunity within the awareness of the person reading. What you do with that space or opportunity is beyond my control. I am helpless to determine that. Whether you let it become overgrown again, whether you plant the seed of some new belief system or whether you learn to keep that space within the forest of your mind empty always is something you alone will determine.

My words are not about knowing. They are about unknowing. I am an iconoclast. I am compelled to tear down cherished beliefs. I am driven by revulsion as much as I am driven by love. But I am a fool. Make no mistake. I am a fool. Because I don't know why I do what I do. I don't understand it. I am simply compelled by some force I can neither fully perceive nor understand.

I am humbled by my own insipid intelligence, by my glaring incomprehension. I look at a wasp sitting on my windshield as I write this and I'm blown away by the complexity yet utter simplicity of this phenomenal creature. And I have no idea what it is, how it comes to be. And beyond the wasp, I look at this world: the rice farmer spraying his fields with pesticide, pale blue mountains under cumulonimbus clouds pregnant with rain, two dragonflies locked in fornication as they soar above the power lines. I am amused and astounded by my profound ignorance.

What a deeply stupid creature I am! Seeing this used to depress me once upon a time. Now it only makes me laugh. I have no desire to know anymore. Because I simply can't know. I'm an innocent idiot. And seeing this has freed me to just *be*.

I can't tell you what any of this is. What a wasp is. It's beyond description. Far too sublime to articulate with vulgar words. What is a wasp? What is a cloud? What is this world? What is life? I can't articulate any of this.

The truth is there. Right in front of my eyes. I can see it! I *am* it! But I don't know what it is. I can't tell you what it is. Yet 'knowing' what it is simply doesn't motivate me anymore. However, what I *can* tell you is that it isn't what you say it is. Whether you are a scientist or a spiritualist, I can tell you that you don't know the wasp, you don't know the cloud, you don't know life. You don't know shit. And I can write tomes about what you don't know.

But I can't write a single word about what I *do* know. Because, I don't know shit either.

All I can do is hack at every false belief, every nonsensical piece of speculation, every assumption taken for granted as fact. Hack, hack, hack, hack. In order to open up a space in a mind dense and overgrown with weeds. A space for you. A space for me. A space for anyone who wants to see. Because I have found that sanity exists only in this space.

I use words to combat other words. But my words, taken out of the context of such combat, are worthless, flaccid, foolish things turning me into nothing more than…

A wolf howling at the moon.

A dog barking in the wind.

An imbecile speaking in tongues.

Make no mistake.

The Tao I speak, is not the real Tao.

Books in print from New Sarum Press

Real World Nonduality—Reports From The Field; Various authors

The Ten Thousand Things by Robert Saltzman

Depending on No-Thing by Robert Saltzman

The Joy of True Meditation by Jeff Foster

'What the...' A Conversation About Living by Darryl Bailey

The Freedom to Love—The Life and Vision of Catherine Harding by Karin Visser

Death: The End of Self-Improvement by Joan Tollifson

2020 Publications

Glorious Alchemy—Living the Lalita Sahasranama by Kavitha Chinnaiyan

Collision with the Infinite by Suzanne Segal

Transmission of the Flame by Jean Klein

The Ease of Being by Jean Klein

Open to the Unknown by Jean Klein

Yoga in The Kashmir Tradition (2nd Edition) by Billy Doyle

The Mirage of Separation by Billy Doyle

Looking Through God's Eyes by Han van den Boogaard

The Genesis of Now by Rich Doyle

Fly Free by Dami Roelse

www.newsarumpress.com

Made in the USA
Middletown, DE
11 November 2020